Canal Cannot

or

The Ecstasy of Being

by
Rod Taylor

Friends I have made
unlivable with women I have known
battles with British Waterways
A saga of travelling round the inland
waterways of England
looking for the perfect woman
painting canal ware, building boats and
busking

Canal cannot

		page
chapter one.	A new life.	3
chapter two.	Ghost.	10
chapter three.	Boating busking and boozing.	32
chapter four.	Roland & Marilyn.	45
chapter five.	Tarleton.	59
chapter six.	The Black economy country	67
chapter seven.	Back to Yorkshire	76
chapter eight	Rickmansworth	87
chapter nine	The road to ruin	92
chapter ten	Cannot sell here	112
chapter eleven	Again	117
chapter twelve	First Blood	125
chapter thirteen	May, Queen and I	136
chapter fourteen	Barred not Bard	152
chapter fifteen	Flying testosterone	164
chapter sixteen	Rallying to the cause	182
chapter seventeen	Stratford again	188
chapter eighteen	All at sea with Wylam	198
chapter nineteen	All at sea again	219
chapter twenty	Boat hooks at dawn	224

chapter one

a new life

"Greg has offered to pay you to join the band! - I don't believe that." Sally exclaimed with incredulity,
"I have been to lots of gigs with them and joined in for absolutely nothing, that is just not fair!"
Sal was tall, dark haired with deep brown eyes and strikingly beautiful gypsy features. It was both the first time and also the last time that he was ever paid, or even asked, to join in because they had rather rapidly discovered that his attempts at stomping along with his 144 bass piano accordion were not only out of tempo but also in the wrong key.
"I'll write some music out for you." Greg offered him with a hint of sarcasm.

Rod and Sal had ended up in Runcorn after the Christmas boating rally and had been offered a 45ft cut down 'Walkers Ricky' - canal boat parlance for a boat built by the Walkers boat yard in Rickmansworth. It was a wooden narrowboat called 'Kew' for a snip at only £400. It was a bit rotten but had a working engine and an old piano on board. That was about it except for a small gas cooker and a bucket, for the use of! It did also boast of a home made solid fuel stove made out of a gas bottle with a door cut into the side where the fuel went in.

It was nearing the end of February and the ice was beginning to melt on the canal so they decided to boat on to Middlewich and moor below the 'Big Lock'. All went well until they set off after a lunch break at the Broken Cross.
"What are you doing?" Sal shouted at Rod who had suddenly turned left off the main canal and was crossing a 'flash', bouncing over the half sunken barges in the larger of the 'flashes' near Northwich.

A flash, is a deep lake caused by the ground sinking into ancient Salt mines. In this particular one there had been many working narrowboats intentionally sunk when the trade had died on the canals. The working narrowboats had been sunk to preserve them so that they could be re-floated when trade picked up again. That had never happened but these relics of a bygone age were now being hauled out to be re-floated and restored as leisure craft and house boats.

"The ice has cut a hole in the bows and we are sinking fast. Just look inside!" Rod yelled - Sal did and could see the water rushing through the boat. It had already covered the piano legs. Rod accelerated towards the far side of the

flash where there was an improvised muddy slipway which had a couple of recently rescued hulks waiting to be restored. As their progress was slowed down by the sunken wrecks, Sal shouted above the noise of the engine and crunching of wood.
"You should just let her sink here with the other wrecks, I don't know why you bought her anyway! She is just a waste of money!"

As the sinking boat hit the slopping bank at the far side of the flash Rod jumped up on to the roof, ran down the full length of the boat grabbing the front rope as he jumped off. He just managed to tie Kew up on to a recently salvaged working boat to prevent her sliding back into the water.
"Stop being so negative.." Rod implored, "...and start pumping the bilges while I go and find something to patch the hole with" he shouted, with frustration, as he set off across the fields.

He eventually returned with tar, roofing felt and a galvanized sheet of metal. It was a brilliant improvised patch and they set off the following day navigating a careful path round the sunken sister ships. They had left Sal's small pontoon named the 'Shed' at Middlewich after going to Tarleton on the Christmas rally. Shed was a cross between a shed and a gypsy caravan on water. It was painted maroon and had gold scroll decorations. They planned to live on Shed while Rod fitted out the Kew to make her habitable.

-

Before the rally and just after Rod had left his wife and family, unable to resist the overwhelming love which he had for Sal, He had moved in to Shed with her on the Trent and Mersey canal. It had been a mad, mad incredible time with sex like he had never known before in the whole of his life. It was all consuming but also frustrating at times when Sal was too tired. She would go to sleep and he would lay awake all night with an
 unbearable hard on. These occasions were rare but it was even more frustrating, after one of these nights that she would wake up refreshed and eager to make love to him only to find that his willy had become weary and floppy after the nights denied eagerness.

Shed was powered by a small Seagull, not the bird, but an outboard engine with as much power as a lame seagull. They gave themselves two weeks to do what should have been a the three day trip with a maximum speed of 2mph with a tail wind or actually going backwards with any kind of a head wind. It took them nearly the two weeks to get half way there   partly because they would take several breaks a day to make love.
"You like having sex as much as I do" she would say as they engulfed each other in one joyous ecstasy of being.

Shed was pinned firmly to the side of the Bridgewater canal by a strong side wind when friends of theirs, Pam and Malk, caught them up in their traditional wooden work boat and thankfully took them in tow.
"Where is the turkey, the stuffing and the onions?" Pam was panicking after they arrived at their destination. There had been several boats moored up at Worsley on their way down and it would seem that some rubbish had been put

on top of the bag with these items in and the whole lot had been thrown in the skip at the dry dock in Worsley.

"Mike is coming from there and he has not set off yet" John said, "Phone him up and see if he can find them". This was done.

When he arrived a couple of days later without the Christmas fair which he had not been able to find, he was furiously amused.

"Which bastard phoned the police to say that they could see an intruder raiding the Worsley skips in the middle of the night?" he asked knowing that the practical joker would probably not own up. Everybody ate together and after the meal Pam owned up to the phone call and also to the fact that she had dropped the replacement Christmas pudding into the canal and rescued it.

"Its been well steamed since then" she assured them.

The destination of the rally was to moor up outside the house of some boating friends where they had planned to hold a big party. The party was in full swing with the Boat band and everybody with an instrument was busking along when Pam pointed to the glass door which went through to the kitchen. Sal and John were hard at it with her on top going like a steam hammer.

"That's the way to do it" Pam applauded as everybody tried to watch the action.

Rod was not too pleased and after a stiff whisky went out and sat in a tree next to Shed for a couple of hours with Sal trying to persuade him to come down.

"Its only a quickie", "John and I always have a shag when we meet up. It doesn't mean anything!" she tried to explain. It was a steep learning curve, this new life of his,

and it was not a matter of forgiving her it was a simple matter of accepting this new reality.
After the celebrations they were towed back to Northwich by Edd with his coal boat. Edd was a high powered banker or something like that who enthusiastically maintained the old working boat and delivered coal to boaters along the canals in his spare time.
"Take over for a bit whilst Sal and I do a bit of catching up" he said as he and Sal vanished into the back cabin. This seemed a bit strange because they could have easily continued chatting on the back deck as they had already been doing.
"My insurance!" exclaimed Edd as he shot out of the cabin after his fully laden barge had bounced off a steel cruiser moored on the outside of the sharp right hand bend just after Burscough.
"It's a good job it was steel" he observed as he looked back to see what damage had been done.
 "If it had been wood or fibreglass we would have cut straight through it!"
It was his first time at the tiller of a barge and Rod had made the classic mistake of trying to slow down on the bend instead of powering and pumping the rudder round it. Edd took over the steering after that and whether the 'chat' between Sal and Edd had been concluded he will never know! He towed them as far as Northwich which was where his moorings were and they continued under seagull power to Middlewich. It was a couple of days after that when they got a lift to Runcorn to look at the old wooden narrowboat called Kew which was for sale.

The Middlewich rubbish skips were only about half a mile down the canal from where they were moored. It amazed both of them how much really good stuff people threw away rather than take it to a charity shop. This was in the late 80s before the Council put up security fences round the skips. They joined other gleaners in rescuing valuable objects which angry deserted husbands or wives had thrown their unfaithful partners belongings away.

"Hey! Look at this", said Sal one day as she found a box of jewellery, "and here's a tool kit for you!" There were men's shirts, still in their wrappers, children's clothing and lots of other really good stuff. Over the period of a couple of months Rod fitted out Kew with a shower-bath, sink, kitchen units and there was enough free wood to build everything they needed.

chapter two

ghost

Sal was still doing one evenings modelling a week and it was on one of these dark misty evenings in early spring when Rod was driving up Finneys Lane to collect her from the station in their battered Renault 4 when out of the mist from a field over to his left, in which he knew there was a riding school, a horse and rider jumped over the hedge straight into his headlights. The horse's nostrils flared a great steamy exhalation of breath behind which he could see the rider who was wearing a brown cloak and wide brimmed black hat.
"Stupid bugger!" Rod shouted aloud to himself as he braked hard at the same time as throwing the steering wheel to the right so violently that the engine stalled. Visibility was very poor so it was lucky that nothing had been coming the other way.

"How the hell! Did it not land on the bonnet of the car?" he thought to himself as he got out to remonstrate with the rider. Silence, not a sound could be heard. Nothing could be seen. There was no sound of receding horse's hooves, nothing. He could even hear his own heart beating. The extra chill in the air made his hair stand on end as though he had seen a ghost.

"I need a drink!" He said to Sal explaining what had happened as he drove her back to the boat after picking her up from the station. They went into the 'Newton Brewery' which was only a few hundred yards from where the incident had happened. As he was being served he related the events to the landlord and a couple or locals who were seated at the bar.

"That's 'Finney!' one of them said and the others nodded in agreement. "He was a highwayman who was shot dead in act of holding up a stage coach.

"He is seen quite often. It's where the lane got its name from!"

The next day Rod went to look at the spot where it had happened. The hedge was thick and overgrown to the height of some 20 feet. There was no way that a horse could have jumped over or through it. He now knew that, 'whatever anybody said', he had seen a ghost.

Rod still had his part time teaching jobs in Keighley and was staying at the family home with Belinda, his estranged wife. He was now, not only staying at the Hall, but Bel had taken him into her bed again. She was in denial of the fact that he had left her and was pretending, to herself, that Rod was just working away most of the week. He was quite happy with the arrangement and Colette, their five year old daughter, was ecstatic with the illusion that her parents were back together again.

Sal was not altogether happy about his dual role.

"It's been me, in the past, who has usually had a few men on the go at the same time!" She observed. "But! I love you! It's like living with a comfortable old sock; you are so easy to be with!" Rod was not sure about the, back handed, compliment but he had known her long enough to be pretty certain that her stories of previous relationships were true. One evening they had compared how many cars he had crashed which ended up at the wrecker's yard to how many men she had wrecked. The score was 14 each.

The 'Big Lock' pub was a rambling Victorian building overlooking the lock below which they were moored. It had a stable block attached to it which was empty. The pub itself was open but, except on rare occasions, was the least friendly pub they had ever come across. The landlord and landlady could be amongst the best hosts at these rare times and the beer would also be in good condition. The rest of the year it was like going in to a house of horrors with vinegar for beer and an attitude to the customers, which even Basil Faulty could not emulate, consequently nobody frequented it. Rod approached the brewery and persuaded them to rent the stable block to him for a very small fee. It seemed a perfect place for a canal side craft and junk shop. There was no separate electric or water supply to the stables so Rod asked the landlord if he could have a metered supply of water and electric from the pub. The request was refused in as ungracious a manner as could be imagined.

Sal chose the name, 'Junk and Disorderly' which described it perfectly. After they had tidied it up and whitewashed the walls and ceiling they fitted it out with tables and shelves from the skip. The main stock was hand-woven rugs, clothing and fabrics which were left over from Rod's craft business. The rest of the stock was a variety of antiques and bric-a-brac from the skip. Without electricity the place was too dark and gloomy for even the hardiest passers-by to venture in, so although it had been fun to do it was a resounding failure.

Some years later when he called at the pub it was humming with life and the stables had been opened as a restaurant. The same couple who had made the place so inhospitable had bought the failing pub from the brewery at a knock down price and were now making it into a great success. What a business plan! During this 'Junk and Disorderly' phase of their relationship they booked in to a couple of antique fairs so that Rod could sell some of his collection of textile pieces. He had a couple of, hand operated, brass winding machines, old sewing machines and a circular bed knitting machine amongst other textile related collectables. They also took some of the hand-woven rugs and shawls which were left over from his weaving studio.

At the Nantwich fair he also took his Father's old Smith and Wesson 6 shooter antique pistol. It was one of the first items he sold to a fellow stallholder who specialized in old armor, guns and associated antiques. The hall in which the fair was being held also doubled as a theatre and their stall was immediately below the stage. They were still madly in love and took any opportunity to make love. Rod went to explore the stage and signaled Sal to join him behind the curtain. It was one of their 'things', to make love in as many different locations as possible so the stage was a perfect place. The curtain was not raised on them, but, as another stall holder commented later the sound of them raised a bit of a cheer.

During their relationship, on instructions from Sal, he never wore shorts. "They get in the way of having instant sex", she said, saying that she would not wear knickers either. One day when they she was sitting on his knee with a long dress on, on a crowded train, They managed to spend most of the journey in a long very satisfying orgasm. When they returned to the stall a woman wanted to buy one of the old sewing machines if they had needles to fit it. Rod went out round the town to but failed to find a shop which sold them. On his return Sal told him that the police were looking for him and had left him a note to contact them at the police station after the fair. He went into the police station and was promptly arrested for 'Gun Running' in Nantwich. "But, it's an antique, it's been spiked!" Rod tried to explain. "I used to play with it as a child and my father spiked it to make it unusable".

They eventually let him off with a caution explaining that it could easily be re- commissioned and that the only antique guns which he could posses without a licence ware flintlocks and the like but nothing which took a cartridge.

It could not last! Such a love as Rod had for Sal was bound to result in too many 'banana skins of life' with nearly all of his attempts at making a living on the canals coming to nothing. Sal had fallen in love with Rod as the 'alpha male' and could not cope with this confused person who she now found herself with. The bottom had fallen out of his world by his act of leaving his wife and family. It was as though he was falling through the bottom of a bottomless bucket into a black hole.

"Sal, I will need a bit of support to get through this" he started to explain to her but before he could continue she interrupted with a lengthy diatribe saying that she was fed up to the teeth with having to support men and why didn't he get divorced and half of the money from his precious mansion or go back to his wife.

"Not financially" he tried to explain, "Emotionally" but it was to no avail, in her eyes he had become yet another looser in her life which was full of useless men.

"I'm pregnant" she announced one afternoon in March after going to the doctors. This revived their relationship and, for a while happiness reigned. Rod severed all ties with his estranged wife and committed himself to a new family life. A month later Sal had a miscarriage. They were devastated and although he did not realize it at the time it was the beginning of the end of her love for him.

It was a difficult time and brought back, for her, memories which she had tried to forget. She had been pregnant once before when she was in a serious relationship with a lad from Liverpool. Sal had never used contraceptives because she had always wanted children but had thought that she was infertile because it never happened. The tragedy of this was that she had been working away for a few weeks and had sex with another man during that time. She told her partner that she was pregnant and they were both delighted until she realized that the child would not have been his. Without telling him, she had the pregnancy terminated.

"It might not be yours and I could not go through with the thought that it might not be" she explained as though it made perfect sense. He was a staunch Catholic.
"Didn't it occur to you that I might have had something to say about it?" was his astonished reaction. She had made bad mistake. He would not even try to understand, and even less, forgive her. That was the end and he walked out of her life.

Up until then Sal had never talked about her past. To her it was another world to be thrown out with the rubbish. It seemed that the loss of another chance to have children brought past events into sharp focus and she began to tell Rod of things which she had never revealed to anyone. She was the result of her mother having a fling with a Gipsy fairground worker and, for a while had been brought up by her grandmother. Her mother had eventually got married and had children to him before Sal was taken to live with them. Sal was treated badly by her mothers husband and also abused by him. She was then fostered and abused by her foster father.
"He was a lovely loving man" she explained without any malice.

Her mother was then divorced and she went back to live with her and her half brothers and sisters. She was encouraged to go to church and at the age of 14 had an affair with the Vicar. Their illicit affair was discovered and the Vicar was defrocked. She was fostered out for the second time to a family in Somerset. After being abused again she eventually ran away to start her semi nomadic life doing whatever jobs she could find before training as a nurse. After that she worked with various street theatre groups where she had learnt to play the melodeon.

They had been talking about travelling the canals and inviting other Thespians to join them on Kew doing 'Boating, busking and boozing' holidays, so, before they finally parted company she helped him to finish fitting the narrowboat out for that purpose. They decided to head for London where Sal wanted to enrol on a course at a mime school.
"Ok!" said Rod, "We will go the long way" she agreed. He hoped that a three week trip might help her change her mind about splitting up.
A few days later they set off up to Wigan with Shed in tow retracing that part of the journey which they had done so slowly and passionately whilst heading for the Christmas rally. They still made love but he was by now, even more of an emotional wreck, and suffered from something which he had only heard of other men of less sterner stuff than he thought he was. Erectile dysfunction!
"Stand up you bugger" he would remonstrate.
"Don't worry" Sal would say, "It happens to a lot of men".
'Probably,' he thought 'When you have finished wrecking them'
The long way to go from Middlewich to London was to go over the Leeds Liverpool canal, up the Trent, up the River Soar and down the Grand Union. It was a fascinating journey and several friends joined them for a few days at a time. As they approached Keadby on the Trent, lock keepers and other boaters were very dubious about them taking Shed on that part of the tidal river.
At Keadby the lock keeper was even more sceptical.
"If you get in to trouble, just cut it loose" he advised.
"Let's go back the other way" Sal moaned at the thought of losing her home. Rod would have non of the negativity

and the next morning they were locked out on to the raging torrent of the incoming tide in between laden barges passing the canal entrance on their way to gravel works near Cromwell lock. Rod had put Shed on short cross straps so that it followed the struggling Kew more easily. They made Torksey by mid afternoon without much trouble except for the last mile or so when the tide had turned which slowed them down considerably. They decided to stay there and catch the tide the following day.

'Why do people always do this?' Rod thought to himself as Sal and Pete ganged up against him for taking them on to the river. Peter was an old friend of Rod's who had joined them for a few days boating.

"We got here ok! Didn't we?' he raised his voice back at them that evening as they walked the short distance to the nearest pub. After a couple of drinks and some pub grub the mood was better but on their return to the boats Sal did not want his attentions and he could not sleep. At about 1am he got out of bed and started the engine.

"What are you doing?" Sal asked sleepily. Pete appeared and swore at him for being woken up.

"We are going on the night tide" Rod asserted as he cast off. "There is a good moon and we have a chart". As they swung left out of the canal entrance a cruiser came round the corner inward bound from Keadby.

"Where are your nav. lights?" the skipper shouted as he was blinded by Kew's spotlight. "I'll report you to the navigation Authority" he shouted again as he narrowly missed them.

"Him and his fancy cruiser with its flashy fairy lights" Rod muttered loudly.

"They're navigation lights" Sal shouted at him, "You are supposed to have them on tidal waters" He knew that but was just being obtuse.

That did it! Sal and Pete really laid into him and to confound it even further they then went aground on a sand bank a few hundred yards further up stream.
"It's ok!" Rod assured them, "...we will soon get washed off; the tide is coming in". It was light by the time they reach Cromwell and the lock keeper told them that he was supposed to detain them for travelling at night without navigation lights.
"It's ok" he told them, "It's not my job to arrest people" he said as he opened the top gates and waved them goodbye. Rod slept whilst the crew boated on to Newark where Pete jumped ship. They never heard any more about incident with the sea-dog in the night.
The trip went ok until they reached the Grand Union when Rod decided to shave his beard off and stop smoking.
"You have a classically wonderful chin!" Sal almost salivated. "It's usually chinless wonders who grow beards to cover them up" she went on as they managed to have sex whilst Rod was still, if somewhat waveringly, steering the boat. The bonhomie did not last and when Sal deserted him, leaving him to do the locks single handed, whist she helped a boat load of horny lads in a hire boat to do the locks behind them, he lost his rag and walked off down the towpath shouting at her to take over because he had had enough. Later that day when she had eventually caught up with him at the Crystal Palace pub he had bought some cigarettes and was puffing away quite happily over a pint. Sal had brought the boats down the

rest of the locks by herself and had scribbled in their journal,
'Rod is taking a day off to infuriate himself'

It was not working. Their relationship had floundered on the rocks of disillusion. Sal helped him to finish the boat off with loose covers on the sparse furnishings and some brightly coloured curtains. The sleeping arrangements comprised of a very large double bed in the front cabin. The smaller middle section had a shower bath at one side and a chemical toilet whilst at the other side there was a single bunk bed. In the main cabin there were two bench seats, the backs of which, hinged up to make bunks, thereby sleeping four more people. The piano doubled as the kitchen work surface and the sink and small gas cooker filled the rest of the space.
Rod was moored up in Camden and had a notice in the window advertising for crew to take Kew to Middlewich. He was not short of offers and eventually selected a Canadian girl who was back packing round Europe called Leslie. An out of work executive who had been made redundant resulting in his wife divorcing him and his mistress dumping him. David also had a tape recording with him to play before sleeping which was supposed to help him to regain his self confidence. Richard was recovering from a bad motorbike accident and, although he had a limp seemed to be well on the way to recovery. Annette in her mid 20s was a similar age to Richard and by sheer coincidence it turned out that they knew each other. It also turned out that she was also recovering from something. A sexually transmitted disease and was on strong antibiotics. The final member of the crew was Celeste who was in her mid 40s and just a bit mad.

"You go off and shag around to forget me!" Sal told him as she waved them goodbye. Rod decided to head down to Limehouse and take them on a trip of a lifetime up the tidal Thames to Teddington and from thence to Oxford and north from there.

It was a bit stressful going down the locks with a crew who had never been boating before and although Rod thought that he was just instructing them he found that he had a mutiny on his hands after they had passed through the Islington Tunnel and were about to enter the next lock.
"That's it!" Richard firmly addressed Rod, "I am not going to be shouted at like this!, I am leaving". A couple of the others concurred with Richard and it looked for a while as though the trip was ending before it had begun. Rod was rather taken a-back as he had to shout the instructions over the noise of the engine.
"Sorry!" Rod apologized and agreed that he would try to explain in more quiet terms what they had to do. It was a kind of ice breaker and after stopping at the next pub for a drink and a bit to eat they continued to Limehouse more harmoniously.

The financial arrangement was that they would all contribute a few pounds a day to cover the cost of food and fuel and also that they might like to do a bit of busking for their beer money. The trip up the Thames was not without incident and Rods attempt to stop at a fuel barge just before Tower Bridge resulted in failure. Kew was swept past at great speed and headed for a bridge peer. Disaster was averted as Rod powered Kew round the obstacle and they bounced about like matchstick in the wake of the trip boats and commercials through the turbulent Pool of London.

It was Rod's first trip up the Thames and in an attempt to find out where to buy diesel he attempted to stop on the wharf at Chiswick Quay marina but they were told that no diesel was available there. The propeller caught on a rock as they steered away. They had to continue in the hope that they would not run out of fuel. After that incident there was a noticeable juddering as they steered Kew but it did not seem to be causing a problem at that time. They moored up just above Teddington lock for the night and after sharing the task of preparing and eating food they all went to a local pub in good spirits. It had a sign outside offering two for the price of one in their new sauna. After a couple of drinks they all decided that it would be a good idea to take up the offer. It was a riot! They were like school kids who had been left unattended by their teacher.

It had started sedate enough with them all sitting with their towels modestly covering themselves until one of them, nobody could remember who, whilst splashing the water on the coals, thought it would be fun to be more generous and splash the rest of them with the cold water at the same time.
"You rotten beggar!" Annette exclaimed dropping her towel and chasing Richard into the cold shower cubicle after he had splashed her. Everybody joined in with the fun and romped between the sauna, the hot room and the cold showers towel less with gay abandon laughing hysterically, probably at the relief of surviving the trip up the Thames. As on the previous night Richard and Annette had slept in the double bed whist the rest of them had the bunks.
"No, no! we can't" Not until I have finished the antibiotics Annette could be heard whispering to a frustrated Richard

whilst the others remonstrated with David for playing his tape too loud.

The next night somewhere a bit further up the Thames after they had eaten and Rod had gone out to buy some milk, they had all dressed up in his various busking costumes.

"Let's go to the pub and play some music", they chorused on his return so when he had found a few bits of costume they piled out into a pub garden. After an hour or so Rod excused himself saying, and meaning it, that he would have to go and check on the stern gland before he had had too much to drink.

"I'll come with you" Leslie said, "I could do with a walk" As they walked back they took each others hands and in the short time it took them to get back to the boat they were embracing passionately.

"I didn't think you were interested in me" she confided as they took possession of the double bed. 'Silly girl' he thought to himself, and said out loud,

"Of course I fancied you but you are 25 years younger than me and I did not think there was a chance of you fancying me".

When the rest of the crew returned and observed the situation, Celeste let out a little scream and nearly fell of the back of the boat for reasons which were only to become clear later.

The following day, Richard was out on the back deck taking a turn at steering when he shouted at the others who were variously either on the front deck or sunbathing on the roof to come and look at a strange phenomenon.

"Look! It's a flying fish!" he exclaimed pointing out at something behind them. Not only did it look like one flying fish it looked like a few of them following each other as they splashed in and out of the water in an amazingly straight line.

"Woah, woah, woah" shouted Rod as his eyes followed the skimming line which was attached to a fisherman straining at his rod some hundred yards behind. "Stop!" but it was too late and the fisherman fell over backwards as his line snapped cursing the boat who's propeller had fouled his line.

"I think you went a bit near the side back there" observed Rod as the fist shaking apparition vanished out of sight when they went round a bend in the river. Rod was nearly always up at the crack of dawn and had set off before any of the others had woken up. Celeste who did not like to miss anything was usually the next to get up and always joined him on the back deck. She never stopped talking.

"Don't you ever stop talking?" asked Rod one morning as she was beginning to annoy him.

"My friends and I always talk at the same time". "We can get more information across that way" she went on, and on and on so that eventually he stopped trying to listen and it became just an adjunct to the sound of the engine. During this part of the journey Rod and Leslie as well as Richard and Annette were all four of them sleeping in the king size bed in the front. This was even more frustrating for Richard who was still being kept at arms length whilst the other two were bonking away quite oblivious to everything. During the quieter moments the conversation between David and Celeste could be heard.

"Would you like me to make you a cup of tea?" he offered when neither of them could sleep because of his therapy tape.

"You won't get into my knickers with just a cup of tea" she protested.
"How about a whisky then" he offered, "it's probably far better therapy than this tape anyway" he admitted.
"Ok!" "But the answer is still the same", she said accepting the whisky.
When they reached Oxford they decided to stay for a couple of days. On the morning of the first day they all got dressed up in his costumes again and went out busking. It was great fun, the whole trip since the mutiny had been like a group of old friends going out on a reunion. Leslie decided that it was time for her to continue with her travels and as the five of them set off towards Dukes cut and the Oxford canal she waved them goodbye. Celeste was not very good at steering and put them aground a couple of times one of which resulted in the propeller picking up a tent from the shallows near the side of the canal. The steering and the whole boat juddered more after that than it had done before. They stopped in Banbury for water where most of them went shopping except for David who they left to look after the boat and fill up with water.

When they returned, Rod was horrified to see David standing on the back deck talking to someone on a boat which had moored up next to them, completely oblivious to the fact that Kew was almost sinking. Rod wrenched the engine compartment cover up and could see by the turbulence of the water round the engine that it must be coming through where the now unseen, submerged, stern gland was situated. The nuts had sheered and the gland had come completely out with the vibration. He managed to push it back and wedge it so that, after pumping out the bilges they were able to get it to a boatyard to have a new prop shaft fitted.

A couple of days later, both Richard and Annette decided that they were going back home as they had run out of money. The three remaining crew saw them off at the next railway station and walked back to the boat with a slight feeling of emptiness.
When you are on the canals places seem to merge into each other and time convolutes, that is except for operating the locks and when you are steering the boat, its like having hours and hours of doing nothing but with no time to do anything. Its even like that when doing nothing and another person is steering except you do find time to cook sometimes.

The day after losing Richard and Annette they found themselves in very sociable pub and after Rod had done a few tunes on his accordion they settled down to a bit of serious drinking before returning to the boat in a state of merriment.
"Sod sleeping on that bench" Celeste said after they had finished the whisky nightcap. "I'm coming to bed with you"
"Ok!" agreed Rod remembering that he had to obey Sal's orders to shag around and forget her. David was then alone with his tape and his whisky but was heard laughing himself to sleep as the events unfolded.
"Why is it that you can get up so early in the morning after hard days boating, busking, boozing and making love all night?" Celeste asked Rod on the back deck as he set off, yet again, at an early hour.
"And to cap it all you went to sleep last night and kept your erection whilst you slept!"
"Did I?" he said, not having an answer to that one.

"You take over whilst I brew up and do some toast for breakfast" he suggested and left her at the tiller just as David emerged already having done the honours.

"Belinda with my five year old daughter Colette are coming to join us tomorrow for the last three days boating" Rod announced and said that it would be best if they slept in the front bedroom with him. Celeste was a bit put out but said that she did not mind. The day after they had joined them when they were on their way down the locks at Malkins Bank Celeste walked back with Rod to shut the lock gate they had just passed through and when out of earshot of the others she really let rip at him. "You bastard!" she exploded, "I thought that you were just sleeping next to her but I heard you having sex last night"
"That's what we do when we are together" Rod explained, "We are separated but we still like to make love when we are together" Celeste was not a happy bunny but she kept her mouth shut when they returned to continue down the locks.

Bel and David seemed to enjoy each other's company so that when they had moored up in Middlewich they went off together with Colette to find transport back to her car whilst Rod and Celeste set off hitch hiking back to London where they parted company arranging to meet up the following day.

Rod found Sal in a state of despair. She had lost her bar job and had not been able to buy any food for a couple of days so Rod took her out for an Italian and told her all about the trip and how he had obeyed her instruction on how to forget her. This seemed to turn her on so that when they returned to her boat she took him to her bed again and

they made mad passionate love reminiscent of their early days.
He did not keep his appointment with Celeste but he did phone her and say that he had to go up north again on family business. She was furious and practised a few new swear words on him.

Before he and Sal parted company a few days later she confessed to him.
"You know the joint bank account we had?" How could he forget it! When they were first together they had gone to the Nat West in Middlewich and opened a joint account so that her modelling money and his lecturing money could be put directly into it. They had been surprised at the time that the bank manager allowed them to open the account because they put their professions down on the application form as 'Actress and Bishop', but in those days it was very easy to open an account and to get a bank card to go with it.
"Yes", acknowledged Rod, "But there is only a couple of pounds left in the account"
"Well!" continued Sal, "I had to pay the tuition fees for the mime course", "I went to a 'hole in the wall' and it let me take £50 out so I went round the corner and drew another £50 out. At the third machine it gave me another £50 but then swallowed my card when I tried it again" she admitted. "Sorry!" she said protesting that some of it was her money and expecting Rod to be rather cross. All that he could do was to roll about laughing at the shear cheek of her and the inefficiency of the banking system to let it happen. It did leave him with an overdraft to manage and the rent was still due on the stable block.

Sal, had been invited, along with her new friends from the mime school to join one of the teachers for a weekend at her house in Suffolk and invited him to go along with them. There were about 10 of them in the van which they had hired for the trip.
"Let's all tell a brief story of our lives" one of them suggested to pass the time and to get to know each other a bit better. In turn they gave some rather boring accounts of themselves with the odd exception so that when it came to Rods turn he did the Yorkshireman's epilogue of,
"You were lucky to have lived in a house!" "We had to live in a cardboard box next to the rubbish tip" "Cardboard box! You were lucky" and so on and so on.   There was a stunned silence during the first few lines and then a gradual thawing out accompanied by laughter when those amongst them realised that it was a comedy act.

Sal was not pleased. She more or less shunned Rod for the rest of the day. She had been embarrassed by his improvised performance. Rod enjoyed the company of these young people. Sal was the oldest of the pupils so Rod, with his full beard and tall stature some 15 years older than her, was positively ancient by comparison.
On the second day, after it had stopped raining, they all went down to the beach. When he and Sal were out of sight of the rest of the party, just when he thought that Sal had led him away for romantic reasons she suddenly pulled him over violently by his hair at the same time as flinging him round in a mad circle shouting.
"You are a disaster!" "Admit it, you are a disaster!" He could have fought back but all that he did was ask her what she meant as he fought back the tears of pain and

incredulity at this uncalled for onslaught. It only stopped when he cried out;
"Ok! Ok!, I'm a disaster", at which she desisted and walked away without another word leaving him sitting there on the rocks, head in hands feeling as though he had been scalped. They drove back to London on the Monday and topped the excursion off with a drink in a pub garden.

As the group was reminiscing about the weekend there was a general consensus that Rods contribution on the way there was one of the highlights of the trip.
"It was one of the best weekends ever", Sal enthused addressing Rod and giving him a theatrical hug. 'It was a bloody nightmare' Rod thought and wondered if they had been on the same outing. He stayed with her that night and then drove back up north to get on with his life without her.
He missed her more than words can express so a couple of weeks later he drove to London in the hope of a reunion. Shed was not moored where he had last seen her so he wandered along the towpath asking boaters if they had seen her.
"Sal and Eddy, you mean?", "Probably at Little Venice" he was told.

"Don't come in!" she said on opening the door of Shed after he had knocked on it.
"I'm just going out to meet some friends", "I thought that we were friends", he said offering to join her. "Some real friends" she said attempting to push past him. It was on impulse as a result of his hurt feeling and the coldness of her rejection of his undying love for her that made him coolly and calmly push her gently off the back of the boat

into the canal. He walked away leaving a couple of her 'friends' who had just arrived to fish her out of the canal.

chapter three

boating busking and boozing

The adventurous idea of forming a kind of ever changing cast in a travelling canal theatre by inviting people with different talents to join them on his narrowboat, Kew which he and Sal had planned was, Rod decided, going to go ahead despite her dumping him.

After the 'slow boat to Middlewich' escapade and a brief reunion with Sally he placed advertisements in various publications for musicians, Thespians or anybody who thought that they could make an interesting contribution to his 'Boating, Busking and Boozing' sojourns around the canals. He proposed a contribution of £10 a day from them and then that they would all get an even share of the busking money and pub performances. They would also help with all the boating work of lock wielding and cooking.

The first two chaps only wanted to join in with the boating but had no talents and no interest in contributing to any entertainments. They decided on a passage to Liverpool and then to cross the Mersey and join the canal at Ellesmere Port.
"Don't go down to Liverpool" several people advised, "You'll get robbed!"

They were three strapping blokes so they decided that it was not too much of a risk for them. After Aintree it became obvious that the local lads made a sport out of throwing missiles from the bridges as they went under and cycling ahead to do the same at the next bridge. They phoned British Waterways who sent a man to travel with them who also enlisted the help of the police to secure the bridges ahead of them. It was like a military operation.
"There was a lone woman who came down against our advice" the British Waterways man related, "She said that she would be ok and would take photos of any yobs who hassled her". "The next morning she was found tied up in her boat, less all of her possessions including the camera", he concluded. As they approached the locks leading down to Liverpool docks he told them that they would have to moor up and wait until the following day for the lock gears be re assembled.
"We have to dismantle all the winding gear and put it in to safe storage between its occasional uses otherwise it would be stolen and cashed in for scrap!" he explained.

A few days in the semi derelict and hardly used Liverpool docks waiting for the wind and the rain to die down so that they could cross the Mersey sapped the enthusiasm of the crew. One of them jumped ship and the remaining one said that he would also leave if they could not cross or that they retrace their passage back along the canal.

The return journey, after they had to wait again for the lock gear to be re assembled, was uneventful. It was far too wet and windy for any respectable vandal to be, destructively, playing out of doors. As they were returning he checked the mail boxes and found a reply from a lady who wanted to join them. He phoned her from a telephone box, it was before mobiles, and arranged to meet up with her near the swing bridge at Burscough the following day.

The day was a complete contrast to the weather of the previous week and the sun shone warm and welcoming. After passing through the bridge they moored up a couple of hundred yards further on which was as near as they could find a space. At the appointed time he kept an eye on the bridge and saw a taxi draw up on the far side. As he set off towards the bridge he saw a lady get out of the taxi, casually look up and down the canal before talking briefly to a man who was standing there. Before Rod was hardly half way to the bridge the woman strode briskly back to the taxi, climbed in and was quickly driven away. The man she had spoken to was still gongoozling when he reached the bridge so he asked him what the woman had said.
" Oh!, she asked me if I had seen a boat called Kew so I told her that it had passed here a couple of hours ago" "Thanks!" Rod said musing to himself, ' Stupid woman, why did she not just look down the canal, she would have seen them'.

They waited a couple of hours to see if she would return. He found a phone box and left a message on her home phone before they set off again thinking that it would be the last they would see of her. Another two hours later when they were about to tie up for the night near another swing bridge an irate woman accosted them and accused Rod of not keeping to their arrangement. Toby went below to get out of the firing line of the now apparently furious Sylvia. The misunderstanding was soon cleared up when she had calmed down and the boat had been tied up. The three of them went to the adjacent pub for victuals. A pleasant evening was had by all.

The next morning after they had set off and whilst Sylvia, who had volunteered to make breakfast was down below, Toby asked Rod to drop him off at the next railway station.
"She's a dangerous woman, that!" he indicated pointing at the interior of Kew and continued in muted tones. "Just be careful of that one!" He left the ship a couple of hours down the canal where they could see a station not far away.

Rod and Sylvia chatted amicably for the rest of the day during which time he discovered that as well as playing the spoons and having a repertoire of folk songs she was, unusually for a woman, a Morris dancer. Her appearance was somewhat at odds with her demeanour with tightly curled hair and a long flowing dress she had the look of the 'Bunny Boiler' in 'Fatal Attraction' He set that thought aside and enjoyed her company as they ended the day entertaining the customers of yet another very sociable pub. He was particularly impressed that she was also a real ale enthusiast and could recite chapter and verse about most of the brews and their history.

The following day they were standing close together on the back deck with his arm around her helping her to steer the boat. It was not long before the, 'help steering', became secondary to them as they became entangled in a passionate embrace, which, after peremptorily tying Kew up, propelled them eagerly into the forward peak where his double bed was situated. The day after that she asked him if she was still expected to pay the £10 a day.

"No!" said Rod, "I'll add the extra service charges on at the end of the week"

"It should be you paying me" she retorted in a jocular manner. "The Captains word is law" he came back with as they laughed and kissed. He knew that he did not stand a cat in hells chance of actually winning the banter.

As they chatted and boated she told him about her family, of her first husband the father of her two children, Lisa, 18 and estranged from her,

"She is quite evil" she said with more venom than seemed natural, particularly coming from a mother.

"My second marriage only lasted two days. It must have been a record" she continued making light of the statement.

"How on earth did that happen?" Rod asked beginning to wonder whether she was being serious or enlisting sympathy for one of life's bum deals.

"It turned out that he was a violent man with an unpredictable temper". She began and continued, "It was a whirlwind romance and after the wedding we were on a train heading for Cornwall where we had bought a cottage. We were about half way there when without any reason, just as the train had stopped at a station, he thumped me in the face, picked up his suitcase and jumped off the train leaving me with my two young children heading for the run down country cottage. I never saw him again and have

only recently got a divorce settlement of half of the house."
"What a terrible thing to happen" Rod sympathized wondering what the other side of the story might be. She had now bought a house in Ormskirk which turned out to be suffering from subsidence. After a few days boating busking boozing and bonking he foolishly arranged to meet up with her at the Whitby Folk Festival in a few weeks time. She was, he thought, quite good company.

In the meantime he boated back to Tarleton and Harry Mayor's yard where he had decided to rebuild the bows on Kew. The timbers were in a worse state than he had imagined so that by the time he had taken all the rotten wood away there was only one plank left above the waterline and the bow frames needed replacing also not to mention half of the bowsprit.

Before going to Whitby he had bumped into Sally at a steam fair in Cheshire and had offered to collect her and run her to Whitby. It was probably not a good idea to take an ex girlfriend to an event where he was meeting up with a new woman so it was, he felt, understandable that when they met up in a pub, Sylvia was a bit touchy about the situation. Things became even more tense later when he was helping Sal put up her tent for her after helping Silvia with her erection. Although the tents were out of sight of each other and at opposite ends of the camp site Sylvia had sought him out and confronted him.
"You will have to make up your mind, right now", she gave him the ultimatum. "Either come back with me right now or you are no longer welcome in my tent"
With that she strode purposefully away and left him in a bit of a quandary. It was a 'no brainer', He had been

destroyed by Sal's previous rejection of him and could not face the prospect of being rejected again.
"Sorry! But got to go" he said to Sal as he left her with a half assembled tent.
"She's a dangerous woman, be careful!" were Sal's last words to him as he headed out of the frying pan into the fire.

The week went by fairly well except that Sylvia did seem to get a bit jealous of him speaking to other people and was pissed off when he went off with Sal one day to help her buy a bodhran, a kind of Irish drum, as a present for her current boyfriend.
On his return to Tarleton and with Sylvia living only a few miles away the relationship blossomed on a knife edge of passion and pervasive bullying.
"You should make a clean break!" Sylvia constantly advised him. "How can you marry me if you are not divorced?"
"Give it time" he would say, "Belinda is not able to come to terms with a final break yet"

He made it quite clear that he would visit his young daughter Colette whenever he wanted to do so but omitted to tell her that he was living a double life and that his wife treated him as though he was just working away most of the time. Colette was happy with the arrangement and he had to admit that the sex life with his wife was better than it had ever been.

Silvia was even jealous of him going out busking with a friend of his called Alex who played the flute. One evening she met up with him in Preston where they had been busking. He was driving them back but she just went on and on about him caring more about other people than he

did for her. Whatever he said it just seemed to make her worse. The road was a dual carriage way with a wide grass central reservation which had mature trees at regular intervals. In desperation to try and shut her up he drove onto this area and wove around the trees in a wild reckless manner.
"What are you doing?" she screamed at him when she eventually noticed the impromptu obstacle course he was negotiating.
"I am trying to get you to shut up" he shouted back at her as if it was possible! It only made her go on at an even higher pitch so that when they reached her home he just dropped her off and drove away back to his boat.

'That was it' he thought to himself as he lit the fire on that chilly autumn evening. It was about midnight and as he sat there in front of the improvised gas bottle wood burner with his head in his hands feeling relieved that the ill advised relationship had ended, when, there she was a banging on the window.

Silvia stormed into the boat in a fury of indignation after having had to get a bus back to Preston where she had left her car, climb over the security fence to get into the boatyard and stumble through the untidy obstacle course of a boatyard, in the dark, to his boat which was now high on a slipway.
"Don't you just walk out on me like that" she shouted approaching him in a threatening manner.
"I've had enough!" Rod pleaded. "Let's call it a day?" "I'm fed up with having to walk on eggshells with your incessant jealousy of anybody I speak to!"
That was like a red rag to a bull. She went on and on, not saying that she loved him but how she could be the most

supportive of friends but, if crossed, the most formidable of enemies. She just went on and on but he stuck to his conviction that it was the end.

After a couple of hours of her constant mental battering it nearly was the end. She picked up a small kitchen knife and made stabbing motions at him at close range. He put his hands up to fend her off and the knife cut into his hand. "That was your fault!" she accused him. "If you had not put your hand up then you would not have got hurt"
"Ok! Ok!" he capitulated in a state of exhaustion after some four hours of constant mental bullying and now the physical attack. "We will give it another try" mainly to shut her up. She bandaged his hand and they made the kind of intense love which is often the result of an enhanced emotional state.

Christmas was almost upon them when Sylvia received a letter from her daughter asking her to meet up and make up. Rod tried to persuade her to take up the offer and she said that she would think about it.

It was Christmas eve and Rod had to set off early to get a good busking pitch in Ormskirk. Sylvia said that she would join him later after Christmas drinks with her workmates in Southport but also asked him if he could look at the windscreen wipers on her car before he went. "No time!" he said jumping into his car and driving off leaving her in a foul mood. He bagged a good pitch and the contributions were flowing in at a good rate. Lunchtime came and went and there was no sign of his music partner so he dashed across the road to a cake shop and grabbed a couple of doughnuts which were the first things which came to hand.

At about 2pm she arrived, quite merry after a few drinks with her workmates and cheerfully inquired. "Have you had anything to eat?" and offered to get him something. "Thanks" he said, "but I managed to get a couple of doughnuts from across the road".
"Did you get me one?" she asked him.
"Well no!, you were not here", he replied a bit taken aback at her question when he had just been responding to her concern for his well-being.
"You never think of me!" she accused him. "You know I like doughnuts".
"Look after the gear" he requested, "I will nip across the road and get you some.
"It's too late now" she retorted, "You are just selfish" which he resented because he considered himself to be a generous and considerate person.
"Look!" he tried to reason with her, "It could have been a pork pie or anything, you just asked me if I had had anything to eat". It fell on deaf ears and after another 10 minutes or so of her haranguing him about the doughnuts and what the lack of him buying her one represented, she stormed off without joining in the musical performance,

It was after 5.30pm when he returned to her home and as he walked into the house, her son picked up his sports bag and shot out of the back door saying, "Best of luck!", I'm out of here!"
There was no sign of Sylvia so he poured himself a beer and counted the record takings of over £140. Just after he had turned the TV on and settled down in an easy chair to unwind from an exhausting day she came downstairs from the bedroom where he assumed she had been sleeping off the Christmas drinks.

"Have you booked the taxi to get us home after the pub music night in Ormskirk?" she asked him in an aggressive manner, "...and, what are you doing just sitting there drinking and watching TV instead of getting ready?", and before he had time to answer either of those question. "How could you be so selfish, buying yourself doughnuts and not getting me one?"

"Taxi!", "What taxi?" he inquired, never having ordered a taxi in his life. "We can phone one when we want to come home" and before she could come back at him. "You have been at home all afternoon, why haven't you booked one? ...and,", he continued, "Have you phoned your daughter yet?". She replied that she had not done so and had no intention of ever doing so!

"We will never get a taxi now!". "This always happens", she continued, "Christmas is always a disaster, I knew it would be!", "Its all your fault for being so selfish for not fixing my windscreen wiper and not buying me a doughnut, I told you that we had not got the time to have sex this morning"

"Given the choice I would choose sex any time to fixing anything!" he interjected with but her sense of humour had taken a Christmas bypass.

The torrent went on ad infinitum for another two hours during which time the only respite was when her son came back very briefly, took one look at the floor show and immediately vanished again muttering, "Fuck! Not again!" as he slammed the door behind him.

Doughnuts, taxi, doughnuts, selfish, doughnuts, not divorced, doughnuts... until Rod had had enough and made a hurried exit through the front door leaving her in full flow.

He drove back to his boat and hurriedly picked up a few things before heading off back to his family home despite being told not to visit over the festive season. Bel's brother was visiting and, for some unfathomable reason hated Rod, but, it was better than waiting on the boat for another knife attack.
He now understood why Sylvia's second husband had just hit her and jumped off the train never to be seen again. Rod would not have been surprised if she had told him that he had jumped off a moving train.

A couple of miles from home was 'The Herders Inn'. It was nearly closing time but he managed to get himself a pint before the bell rang. Tim, a friend of his, was propping the bar up by himself. He and his wife used to have a fish and chip shop but had with Rod's, cautious advice, made Tim's hobby of restoring old furniture into a full time business with huge success. After catching up on recent events and a couple of pints later with no sign of time being called Tim expressed his admiration for Rod having the courage to leave his wife.
"Everybody would blame me as the bad guy if I left mine", he confided, "...they don't know what its like!"
"The grass is not always greener on the other side", Rod tried to console him as they compared notes about the reason for them both drinking alone in a pub on Christmas eve. They, and a few other stragglers, were eventually wished a merry one, as they were evicted from the warmth out into the cold moorland night. Sandra, Tim's wife was a good looking woman but hard as nails in her business dealings. Nobody knows what goes on behind closed doors and it took Tim another ten years to find the courage to leave her.

Thrushcross Hall was all locked up when he got there so he climbed in through a window which he knew did not lock and crashed out on a couch in the large, oak beamed, hall. "Just keep out of the way" Bel instructed him when she discovered his presence in the morning. With fifteen rooms in the Hall and 15 acres of woodland and meadow, it was quite easy to comply until early afternoon when he was in the kitchen and the front doorbell rang. Sylvia could be seen through the small glass panels in the door so before Bel answered it Rod went off and hid in the old studio. Bel came and found him a short time later.

"She knows that you are here", "You have left you accordion in the kitchen so hiding your car was a bit pointless". He went down to face the music which thankfully was in a minor key and after a short redressing and confirming her suspicion that he had been two timing her she left.

chapter four

roland & marilyn

The rebuilding of the bows on Kew progressed at a good pace. Rod had given up the busking and had signed on so that he could work full time on the boat. Harry realised that Rod was not one of those people who started and never finished a job. He had seen it so many times and had many boats in his yard which were half finished abandoned projects. In his time he had disposed of these in several ways when the owners had stopped paying their moorings and had told him that he could have the worthless hulk in lieu of what they owed him. He had set some adrift on to the tidal river Douglas and one of them he had lifted out of the water with his tractor and put it in the middle of the road not far from the yard. When the police came and asked him about it he denied responsibility for it being there but gave them the name and address of the owner who had to pay someone to cut it up and scrap it.

Harry was getting on a bit and was the third generation to have run the boatyard. The family had originally built some of the wooden Leeds Liverpool shortboats which were 60ft x 14ft. After the demise of the carrying trade the yard had hardly changed and was like a piece of the past preserved in aspic. Preserved is probably not the right word for it, rotting in aspic might be more appropriate. There were two large sheds and lots of outbuildings. The outbuildings which were more like various sized garden sheds were literally falling apart and spewing out their contents of nuts bolts, bits of rusting engine parts and other unrecognisable stuff from bygone years. Harry had a couple of modern containers, where he kept his valuable stock, as well as his house which was also bulging at the seams from yet more old stuff, magazines and working drawings for building the shortboats.

There were three slipways, two outside and one inside one of the larger sheds where the boats were hauled out on trolleys running up old railway lines which vanished into the canal. Along with the assortment of partly worked on boats in the large aircraft hanger like sheds there was a network of pulleys and leather belts which vanished occasionally into a stack of old boards or bits of boats which filled every corner.

It all looked derelict and unusable until one day, when Rod was looking for a 3ft long bolt to hold the bow framework to the stempost, Harry told him to excavate a particular corner of the large shed. After a couple of hours of hard labour Rod had uncovered an unlikely looking piece of machinery to which one of the belts from the rafters was connected by a responding pulley. Harry dusted it down, inspected it, applied a few drops of oil here and there,

grunted in satisfaction, shouted for Sam and bade Rod to follow him to the rear of the building where he uncovered a large stationary diesel engine next to which was a bank of ancient looking batteries. Even at a glance Rod could not believe that they could hold a charge. Harry turned a switch on a large dusty electrical control box and the whole shed slowly ground into action.
"They are silver nitrate batteries, out of old submarines" he told Rod as though he was reading his thoughts, "Last for ever!" he concluded.

The thread was cut from a blank which Harry had dug out from one of his tumble down sheds. "Must repair that shed sometime" he muttered to himself and then shouted, "Sam!" deafening Rods left ear as he called his daft Rottweiler for the hundredth time that day. Harry told him where he could get the trees cut at a timber yard in Burscoe and instructed him on how to work out the spiralling for the bow planks. Harry and Peter, his life long assistant, uncovered an ancient paraffin fuelled steamer from the undergrowth just outside the big shed and tore down brambles which were almost supporting the steambox attached to the shed. To be more accurate, Peter and Rod did the work whilst Harry supervised. It was all a brilliant learning curve and spectator sport as some of the long standing moorers looked on in disbelief at what was happening.

One Saturday morning, out of the blue, an inspector from the DSS called and asked if he could come aboard and have a chat. Rod cordially invited him in and offered him a cup of tea.
"It has been reported that you are earning money busking at the same time as claiming benefit!" the official declared.

Rod realized that the only person who would do that was a woman with a mission.

"Would I be here messing about with my boat on the busiest day of the week?" he posed the question. "If I was doing as the person says: who was it anyway?" He asked interrupting his own flow, "I would certainly be out on the streets on a Saturday morning!"

"Sorry but that information is confidential but I can plainly see that you are not doing as the report suggested". The official went away quite happy that the report had been malicious.

The work on the boat was soon completed and whilst he prepared to set off on his travels again he heard a rumour that the person in charge of boating matters at Wigan Pier was looking for someone to rebuild the last of the wooden Shortboats as an out of the water exhibit. When he got to Wigan and observed the sorry state of 'Roland' which for all the world looked like the skeletal remains of a large whale, he asked what the story behind it was. Marilyn, a large cheerful lady in her mid thirties, the person in charge of all things boating told him the sorry story and showed him a photo of the complete vessel as it was when she came out of the water.

"I employed a certain Tim Dainty to restore her as an out of the water exhibit" she began. "I left him to get on with the job and the next thing I knew was that he had cut all the rotten timbers out and reduced it to the bottom with stunted ribs adorned at each end by the bow and stern sprits which you see now". "That was nearly two years ago and despite asking him to come and restore Roland he evades and procrastinates". She took Rod to a storage basement and showed him the timber and boarding which the inept boat builder had purchased for the job. It consisted of 3/14 inch x 5inch softwood boarding, lots of 10ml sheets of plywood, half a dozen three inch thick, two feet wide planks of hardwood and a few scaffolding planks.

"That lot is almost useless!" Rod explained. "The job needs 2 inch oak planking cut out of selected trees. I might be able to cut the frames out of the 3 inch timbers but the rest is totally unsuitable". They went back to her office and discussed the restoration project in more detail. He left after giving her a time estimate of one year at a fixed price of £10,000 plus materials. She promised that she would put it to the committee and let him know in due course.

After spending a couple of days in Wigan, where the Indian restaurant only served chips with the curries and not rice, "Sorry Sir, but nobody wants rice in Wigan they only want chips", he went home for a few days to get a decent curry in Bradford as well as seeing his family before returning and boating on to Worsley.   The canal at Worsley is bright orange due to the iron coming out of the disused iron ore mine which the Bridgewater canal was built to serve. He moored up on the towpath and spent the next few days repainting Kew.

"HI!" he greeted Rod, "Where does this canal go to? He was a smartly dressed tall dark haired man who had accosted him. Rod had casually observed the man park his car, look around and head in a theatrical casual manner towards his boat. He walked past several other boats who's owners were pottering about in the afternoon sunshine or sitting reading. He could have stopped and chatted to any of these but just made a slow bee line for Kew.

"I have just started a new job with the Manchester constabulary and I am just exploring the area" he explained although it was obvious from the insignia on his jacket and his demeanour that he was a policeman. Rod took this innocent question on face value.

"London that way and Liverpool that way', he indicated thinking that the encounter was a bit strange. The angle of the chat became more questionable as to the officers motives when he began to ask more personal questions about how he made a living on the canals and where he had come from and where he was going.

"I'm just moored up here waiting for confirmation of a quote I have given to rebuild a boat for Wigan Peer" Rod replied without giving any more information about himself. The plain clothed top brass copper thanked him and on conclusion of the 'conversation' marched briskly back to his car and drove off.

"I can be a very nasty enemy!" Sylvia's words echoed in his head. At about the same time he received a summons from the dole office to attend an interview.

"That woman!" he thought, "Is trying to stir up shit in whatever direction she can". He had been sent a questionnaire by the DSS and had answered it in a rather facetious manner which was probably more to do with the interview than anything she had done.

"I see here that you expect to get a job earning £500 per week and that you are not prepared to take just any old job!"

"Yes, that's correct, we are encouraged to be ambitious!"

"That's not good enough", if you are not prepared to take any job which is offered to you we will have to stop your payments"

"Look!" Rod interjected, "There are lots of people desperate to get any menial job". "I would not like to deprive them of one". "I have skills to offer the world!". The interview was terminated.

Rod phoned Marilyn a couple of times only to be told that she was waiting for his quote to be approved by the finance committee. After three weeks of waiting he had finished painting Kew so he boated back to Wigan. After tying the boat up and failing to get through on the phone he politely stormed her office. Fortunately she found his enthusiasm and eagerness to get the job amusing.
"I have just had your estimate approved" she confirmed, "But! I will not give anybody this project without good references".
"I had better get you some references" Rod said, feeling a bit crestfallen and wondering where he could get them from. He told her as much and she strung him along for a few minutes before announcing.
"You would not be in my office if I had not checked up on you and got very satisfactory feedback"
The following day, after sorting out a mooring for Kew in the steam engine arm alongside the trip boat mooring, this amiable, ample, young lady took Rod in hand and made her intentions abundantly clear.
"After the disappointment of the previous restorer" she announced, "I am going to keep a very close eye on your progress".
"That's ok with me", he assured her as she took him to look again at the timber which the previous incumbent had purchased to rebuild Rowland. None of it was much use for the restoration. He asked her if the supervision

extended to running him round in her car to source suitable materials to which she readily agreed.

A trip to the timber mill situated next to the canal at Burscoe where he had purchased the oak for Kew proved successful although a compromise had to be reached because oak would have been too expensive. Larch was the chosen timber to be cut to one and a half inches instead of the 2inch oak which she would have been constructed of originally. The yard had stacks of felled trees of all descriptions piled fairly neatly in mountainous elongated pyramids. Trees were selected with suitable curves for the bows and stern spiralling and long straight trunks for the side planking.

Rod really enjoyed this supervision which had the added perks of being wined and dined. After the third or fourth day of supervising the slicing of the trees to the required thickness and curvature they retired to Kew with a bottle of whiskey.
"How do you feel about having a woman as a boss?" she asked him.
"What do you mean by that?" he queried the statement, and countered. "I am self employed and you are my customer", he teased her.
"I'll show you who's boss!" she said, taking him in hand as he breasted up to her with a knowing inevitability of mutual attraction. "My husband is not interested" she confided, "I have been known to lay next to him begging for his love and attention and he just ignores me as I masturbate to quench my needs"

Rod was only too pleased to help a woman in such distress particularly such an attractive woman whose company he felt totally at ease with. Marilyn, he felt was someone you could take on face value, no hidden agenda and a philosophy which helped her see the funny side of everything. Middle class with a good education she had worked in banking before taking the job of everything boating for Wigan Pier in a brave effort to combine her boating hobby with a well remunerated job. Two teenage children who she adored completed what, on the face of it, seemed to be an ideal life.

"Nothing shocks me" she said emphasizing it by telling him that when she was a volunteer Samaritan the others on the switchboard would put any obscene phone calls through to her to disarm the callers with her wit and charm.

The work on the dead carcase of Roland progressed at a good pace when he took on two helpers. One was a local lad named Paul who had trained as a shop fitter but had been out of work for several months. Rods old friend Peter who was out of work again after flirting with running his own fish and chip shop which had failed, as several of his previous business ventures had done, due to his propensity to treat the takings as pocket money. Pete brought along Emma, his 16 year old fiancée who had been working for him in the chippy. Pete with his small stature and boyish looks could easily pass for a much younger man and certainly did not appear to be 30 years older than Emma.

Rowland was perched on a grassy knoll adjacent to the visitor car park, which served the trip boat and the visitors to the engine house containing the largest working steam engine in Europe. This power house was next to the trip boat canal arm and proved to be very fortuitous. Surplus

steam was released over a drain in the yard behind building so Rod asked the engineer of this gigantic piece of Victorian engineering if he could harness the steam for his planks by constructing a steam box out of some of the useless softwood, over the exhaust.
"Go ahead!" he invited expressing enthusiasm for Rod's endeavours. "Just let me know whenever you want more steam". He offered. This saved the expense of hiring and fuelling a steam maker. A large container had been hired for storage and as a workshop if it rained. Fortunately it was a dry summer so most of the cutting of the frames and then the planks was done out in the open air.

A good routine was established with an 8 am, start for the workers before Marilyn arrived at about 8.30 to assess the progress.
"Don't disturb us", Rod would tell his crew, "We will be 'in conference'," whereupon they retired to Kew and made passionate love before coffee and a nip of whiskey set them up before the hard grind of the day ahead.
"Can you give Emma some paid work?" Pete asked Rod. Emma had been mooching around during the day doing a bit of labouring for Pete but was getting rather bored.
"That's a good idea, she can clean my boat make the teas and cook us a meal for after work", suggested Rod. Emma agreed and £5 a day was settled on. She did brew the teas but never got round to cooking so they carried on going to the local pub which served good food at a reasonable price. Paul went home to his wife and kids although he sometimes went for a pint with them after work.

Back on Kew after an extended tea time drink and a game of pool the trio would play cards or watch TV. Emma took to snuggling up between Pete and Rod. Much to Rod's amusement one evening Emma then snuggled up to Rod and sat on his knee.

"Emma!", "What are you doing?" Pete asked her in a somewhat surprised tone of voice not sure of what to make of the spectacle before him. Rod, on the other hand, enjoyed the wisp of a young lass nestling on to him but kept his hands to himself.

"It's only uncle Rod" she said in all innocence, "You don't mind! Do you Rod?" she gestured to him and he could only agree that he did not mind. The fact was that she was still a child of 16 going on 17 and looked on Rod with his slightly greying beard as a curmudgeonly old uncle and did not relate to the fact that Pete was three years older than him. Pete grudgingly accepted the situation and Rod continued to keep his hands to himself.

A few weeks into this cosy arrangement Rod was getting extremely agitated about the fact that Emma as well as never cooking a meal seemed to be making very little if any progress in cleaning the boat. He dropped the odd hints to Emma and had asked Pete to have a word with her about it. Eventually he shouted at Emma asking her to fulfil her part of the bargain and clean the boat.

"I'm not touching that!" she shouted back at him, "It's filthy!"

"That's why I'm paying you to clean the bloody thing!" he retorted but it still never happened. The combination of the fall out with Emma and the fact that Pete found out that Rod was paying Paul more than him seemed to sour their relationship a bit and when the job was nearly finished Pete asked Rod to lend him some money. Rod refused to lend him money for him to start up yet another business, Pete demoted Rod from being best man at his wedding to just being another guest.

'Probably for the best' thought Rod who had been best man at his first wedding which had ended in divorce.

It was a glorious summer and the sun always seemed to be shining. He and Marilyn became good friends and enthusiastic lovers.

"I've been going to leave him for some time" she confided referring to her husband. She explained that it was particularly difficult because her husband was a senior partner in her fathers business and all the family finances were closely entwined. But... she seemed determined that she was going to tell him and leave him whatever the outcome of their relationship.

So... as the rebuilding of Rowland neared its conclusion she offered Rod the full time job of managing the trip boat and function barge so that they could be together. He turned her offer down because the thought of being driven mad, steering a boat backwards and forwards over the same bit of water day in, day out was his idea of hell. She said that she would join him in his chosen lifestyle to which he readily agreed would be a wonderful thing.

"Anyway" he told her, "When you tell him about us he will stand on his head and be everything you have ever wanted him to be".

"He won't!" she said with great feeling, "He's a bastard and I am going to leave him whatever happens".

The work was almost completed after only four months and the helpers had departed. Marilyn seemed to be distancing herself from him so he asked her.

"Have you gone off me?" he asked feeling the impending loss of her comely loving.
"You wise old bastard! How did you know? Yes I am weaning myself off you! He has done exactly what you said he would do. He has become the man I married again. You are going away and I have family and business connections which would be very messy and hard to break. You still have your wife, go back to her, she obviously still loves you". She concluded her barrage of confused reasoning.

Belinda had visited him for a few days with his daughter Colette during the four months work and he had told her of his ongoing relationship. He had also told Bell about Marilyn.
"How on earth have you found the time to fit that in and do all this work?" Bell asked him with an air of total astonishment in her voice. Marilyn, similarly thought it a bit odd that she, his mistress, had been asked and had supplied free tickets for his wife and daughter to visit the various Wigan attractions.
"Well... it's best to tell you the things as they are" he naïvely told them both, separately.
Colette particularly enjoyed the Wigan Pier museum and the re-enactments of life from the early part of the 20th century. She liked the schoolroom with the strict teacher caning pupils for dirty finger nails or talking in class. She was also enthralled by the small slate tablets which they were given to chalk their work on. Rod told her that he had the same slates to work on in his first class at school and that the discipline meted out by the actors was just the same as his teachers used to do.
They all found the re enactment of a funeral very moving and were told that the actors took it in turn to play the

part because it tended to depress them. He learnt later that the museum had stopped doing the funeral because the actors found it just too depressing.

Rods visits to the family home became more regular after that and it seemed as though a lasting re union might be going to happen,

chapter five

tarleton

On the conclusion of the Wigan project Rod was solvent and had achieved an income of £500 a week for the four months work. He was tempted to go and flaunt the fact to the woman at the DSS but it was only a passing thought.

He purchased an old car to run around in and a sunken wooden narrowboat from Harry as a restoration project. Part of the deal was that Harry would install a second slipway so that, working together, they would be able to sideways slip the 60ft boat.
"You must be joking!" some of the long standing customers of the boatyard had said, "He's been talking about installing a second slipway for the last 20 years". "He will never get round to it!"
"You can help!" Harry told him when he pressed for this promised slipway. "At the other side of the lane" he

indicated towards a bramble strewn mass of undergrowth beneath the trees which divided the boatyard from the fields beyond,
"There are some railway lines which I purchased for the job a few years ago. Just retrieve them, chip the rust off and we can make a start!"

It was agreed that Rod would get free moorings for a year in return for his help.
Digging into the scrub, under which the mythical railway lines were supposed to be, was a herculean task and at first he thought that Harry had imagined their existence. When he did eventually dig them out it took Rod two weeks to chip the thick, encrusted rust off them until Harry deemed that they were usable. Harry and Peter, with the new apprentice Mike, set about the task of lifting the old slipway and moving it over a few yards in preparation for putting in the second one a few yards away, alongside it. Harry and Peter were the same age and had gone to the local school together as children. Harry had gone away to university and Peter had been taken on as an apprentice in the boatyard. Despite Peter probably knowing more about the practicalities of every aspect of barge building and repairs, Harry would stand over him and supervise his every move at the same time as shouting over his shoulder for the errant Sam. It was a double act, par excellence, much to the amusement of all who observed their industrious antics.

Mike, the young scrawny, 17 year old, apprentice the son of Linda and John, who had a barge in the boatyard, all became good friends of Rod. Everybody in the yard was amazed that the second slipway was being built and some wondered if Rod had been bribing Harry with some kind of 'services rendered' behind one of the tumbledown sheds to have achieved his co operation.

Rod enjoyed his couple of years at Tarleton. He, along with the group, attended night school where they all passed their 'Day Skipper' certificate. A favourite nightly haunt for this gang of merry mariners was the local bowling club, not to play bowls but to enjoy the cheap beer and play cards and dominoes. The domino game in that part of Lancashire was with 9s dominoes so that up to a dozen of them could play, the first to chip out, in a rowdy banter filled circle. The favourite game was 5s and 3s. The club was in a local games league where Rod partnered with Linda won most of their games.

'Waterwitch' turned out to be almost as big a job as 'Rowland' and nearly broke in half as it was slowly hauled up sideways out of the water letting out hundreds of elvers in the muddy soup from the bilges of the boat as a few rotten elm bottoms gave up the ghost. During the restoration of Waterwitch, Bell and Colette had visited him and he became a more regular visitor to his old home. Nina, his middle daughter, with her partner, Stewart, and baby grandson Jed, also went along for a canal trip up the Rufford arm.

After completing the rebuild of Waterwitch he sold Kew to a lad from London with a promise of delivering it. He enlisted the help of three volunteers who had enquired previously about his 'Boating, Busking & Boozing trips. They were Graham, who had just finished at university with a degree in economics, Philip who was taking a break from being a cycle courier in London and Liz who thought it would be a relaxing holiday. Rod's plan was to make the journey in about a week so Liz dropped out at Wigan after a couple of days when she found to her horror that an early start meant dawn at 5am and boating hard all day except for a refreshment break of a couple of pints of beer and then boating until dusk or just after to find a pub to drink until closing time. They did take turns at cooking or making sandwiches and brewing teas and coffees, as well as steering, but they were long days with many of them lock-weal-ding marathons.

"I have never drunk so much beer in my life" said Graham who was just gone 20 and had not really had a childhood due to a sheltered life of sobriety and study. Phil enjoyed the work out and all three of the remaining crew took turns at cycling or running ahead to set the next locks. Rod phoned Steve, the new owner, the evening they got to Uxbridge to tell him to expect them soon.

Steve in his excitement at the impending arrival of his new home had taken his bike by train to Bulls Bridge and had set off cycling to meet them. He cycled all the way to Uxbridge thinking the they had not even set off but was unable to find them. It was not until he returned to Camden late in the evening that he discovered that they had already passed Bulls Bridge before he got there.

"I did not think that you could have possibly made the journey in such a short time" he commented, disappointed that he had missed them but pleased that they had arrived. All three of them became good friends and kept in touch for many years as well as having lots more boating adventures.

Life for Nina, Rod's middle daughter. was not going well. She and Stew were splitting up which Bel found difficult in it's self but the fact that Nina was leaving Jed with Stew and going off to live in some kind of Ashram in Leeds made it doubly upsetting.

"Stewart is depressed and if I took Jed away he might kill himself" Nina explained. They realised that she was not the brightest spark when she decided to practice her massage skills in her flat in a seedy part of Armley which was the 'red light district' of Leeds. When Rod visited her he had a stiff shoulder which she offered to massage. She did not have a massage table and just spread colourful rug on the floor.

"Take your shirt off and lay down there" she instructed. He obeyed her directions and lay face down on his chest. She knelt across him, legs and body in close contact whist she oiled and massaged his shoulders and back.

Whilst the treatment relived the tension in his ailing shoulder it did far too much for him in another region. When she asked him to turn over and spread eagled herself across his body in a most seductive manner it was just too much.

"For Christ sake Nina", he reprimanded her as he leaped up extracting himself from an erotic impulse.

"Is this how you massage your clients?" I don't wonder that you have had to fight off a couple of clients and a close family friend who tried to take advantage of you".

"Pack it up before you get hurt!" he advised her. "Find yourself a room in an alternative therapy centre where there are other people around and get yourself a proper massage table".

She met up with another lost soul, except that they thought that the rest of the world was lost and that they were found. They both changed their names to fit in with the cult they had joined and Nina lost contact with the family for many months. Bronia, on the other hand, had her feet firmly on the ground. She wanted to get a good job and earn some money but was just signing on and expecting the Job Centre to find her some well paid challenging employment.

"Get yourself a job, any job", he advised her. She took his advice and did several waitressing and bar jobs until one day she announced that she was back at the labour Exchange.

"Working there!" she clarified. "It's a useless job..." she said, "...all I seem to be doing is copying forms which could be duplicated a million times faster, but it's a job, a step on the ladder". She had a steady boy friend with whom she was buying a house and all seemed rosy for her.

In the meantime Rod had agreed to buy a rusty old hull of a Yarwood Station boat which was out of the water in Hawn Basin near Halesowen just south of Birmingham. He set off from Tarleton with his busking friend Erick. He was a slight figure with dark curly hair and played the guitar. He particularly liked modern jazz and Stephane Grapelli who was his idol. His ability to bravely go out into busy shopping centres to busk, belied his innate shyness and self doubt.

They had a small narrowboat, which he had named 'Humph!' breasted up to Waterwitch which Rod had fitted out and was delivering it to it's buyer in Dridlington, on their way to Birmingham via the Leeds Liverpool canal again.

All went well until they reached Apperley Bridge in Yorkshire, below the three rise locks and Apperley lane. They were moored just past the swing bridge where Bel had arranged to meet them and leave 8 year old Colette with them to accompany to Leeds. Only a few minutes after Bel had driven off Rod heard, above the loud music which Eric had put on the cassette player, the faint sound of a distant voice calling his name. He switched the music off and dashed outside where he found his daughter in the water hanging on to the sagging mooring rope in the freezing cold March water feebly calling for him. They fished her out and dried her off remonstrating himself for not putting a life jacket on her when she arrived and went to play on the bows of Humph.

"It's a good job mum taught me how to swim last week" she laughed off the near drowning experience. "When I went under the water I remembered not to panic and swam to the side but I could not get out". To her it was just a silly mishap which she could tell her friends about but to Rod, who had rightly commented to Erick,

"Bel would have killed me if she had drowned". He banned loud music on the boat after that so that he could hear if anybody fell in.

Humph, which had been the goat boat of the previous owner and although it had been thoroughly cleaned out, fitted out and equipped with a single cylinder diesel engine, probably still had a lingering smell of goat, but it was delivered to the new owner who, thankfully had no sense of smell.

The, now familiar, river Trent was achieved in one day with Waterwitch's powerful Lister HA3 engine. She even managed to keep pace with the commercial vessels which was commented on by more than one of their skippers as they, very slowly, overhauled her. Louise, Tom and her brother Steven joined them that leg of the journey. Collette had left him at Leeds.

chapter six

the black 'economy' country

No doubt Rod's Yorkshire accent seemed as strange to the people he met in that part of the Black Country around Halesowen as his did to them but he certainly had the impression that they were pretending to be caricatures of themselves. On his arrival at Hawne Basin the first person he met was a middle aged wiry man of about 5ft 9ins in stature. John Rudge greeted him with a friendly smile and introduced himself as the caretaker come dogs body to the Marina. He had not been boating very long but, along with others in the Basin had rebuilt an old boat for his wife and family to live on.

"Don't ask me to empty your Elson" he said in a meaningful tone, "I did one for a visitor the other day and thought the outlet pipe swivelled outwards. Tore the pipe clean off and got covered in shit", he said laughing at his own misfortune.

The next person he met was Richard Hurley. Rod was standing with a tape measure in hand looking at the rusty hulk which he had bought.
"What are you going to do with that?" Richard enquired,
"Haven't got a bloody idea!" Rod answered realizing the enormity of the task ahead.
"I like an honest man!" Richard said, "A Yorkshire man are you?" he stated rather than asked and after a few more minutes of conversation during which Rod realised that Richard was a master boat builder he began to pick his brains as to the best way of tackling the job.
"You're the first Yorkshireman I have met who is not a bullshitter," Richard said in a rather back handed compliment, "You and I will get along fine", he concluded.

The following morning one of the other marina members, who had a boat out of the water, had a delivery of steel arrive so Rod, along with other boaters, leapt out of his boat to help with the unloading. It was what everybody did so that he earned himself more 'Brownie points'.
Richard was in the process of re bottoming a working boat for a customer of his as well as finishing a new build for an old couple, Duggie and Audrey, who were planning their retirement travelling the canals after making their pile in South Africa.

The boatyard was a hive of industry with the almost constant noise of grinding, welding and hammering. Hawne Basin was at the end of a nearly derelict arm of the canal system which the incumbents had rescued by forming a charity. The members of this far sighted group went out regularly clearing obstructions in the canal which were still being dumped by fly tippers, industrial and domestic. The basin was surrounded by old industry and new industrial units. On one side, just far enough away not to bother them too much was a demolition rubble grading unit which, if the wind was in the wrong direction, shrouded them in dust. On the opposite side was a steel mill which had a several thousand ton press which was only operated occasionally but when stamping out its plates, would shake the marina adding to the noises already reverberating. But, like almost everywhere on the canals it was a haven of greenery and pleasantly tranquil in the long summer evenings.

"If I were doing that boat" Richard advised him, "I would cut out the bottoms, most of the sides and that ugly square plated stern which some moron has put on to it and you might end up with a half decent boat". Rod knew that he was right. Crete was a badly neglected rusty old hull which had been badly patched up like a gammy leg with lots of sticking plasters haphazardly covering over corpuscular boils. On Richards advise Rod went out to purchase the required equipment, an oxyacetylene cutting set which was second hand. He was offered an oxygen bottle from one of the lads building his own boat.
"Just let me know if you want another one", he offered, "and put the empty one over there in the bushes with the others". "Why don't you get them refilled?", he subsequently asked as his third one ran out.
"Its difficult enough nicking the full ones out of the Council workshop", "I don't want to get caught taking the empties back", he explained. Rod shrugged his shoulders and, not wanting to be implicit in acts of blatant theft, decided to buy a refillable bottle from another supplier.

He then went to look at an Oxford, oil filled, welder capable of continuous welding which was advertised in a local paper. It was at another steel works across town. A price was agreed on but he was then told that he would have to pay VAT on it.

"It's cash!" Rod said. "I don't know you", said the man behind his office desk.

"Tell you what!" Rod came back with, quick as a flash. "Lets go out for a pint together tonight and then I can come back in the morning and pay cash".

"Tell you what", the man said laughing at his cheek, "It does not belong to the firm, it belongs to Harry in the workshop, go round the back and pay him the cash!"

He then needed a long heavy duty electric lead for the welder and was directed to an electrical wholesalers. The price was eye watering and Rod asked if he could do a better deal for cash.

"Bring your car round the back at 5.30 just as we are closing, I will see what can be done then", he offered. Rod did as he was asked and at the appointed time he found the back of the shop and reversed up to the door. He knocked, somewhat gingerly, not sure what reception he would get. The man came out heaving a large roll of 5 core cable and dropped it into the back of his car.

"£20 quid", he requested looking round shiftily in case they were being observed.

"Thanks!", said Rod as the man vanished back into the anonymous looking door in the shady back alley.

Rod now knew why it was called the 'Black Country', It was the 'Black Economy Country'.

It was even better than that. When the steel was about to be delivered, for cash!, he went down to his bank the evening before and drew £400 from one of his accounts, he then took the card out for his second account and realised that he had put the wrong pin number in but that it had given him the money. He then put his other card in to draw the maximum of £400 out because he needed £800 for the steel. Intentionally, this time, just out of curiosity he put a random four digits in and it obliged him with the money. The next morning he went down to the bank again to see if it would work with any old card but the hole in the wall had an 'out of order' notice on it. Many months later when he did his accounts he realised that neither of his accounts had been debited with the withdrawals.

It was like a firework display, cutting the old rivet heads off and after several burns on exposed bit of flesh, which he thought were out of range of the exploding encrusted rust, he covered every bit of himself from head to toe.
It was a hot summer so that working in what was ostensibly a large steel bath he was constantly drenched in sweat for the entire couple of weeks it took him to cut out all the bottoms and lower sides. Standing 6ft tall and not a heavy built bloke he looked like a figure from Belsen by the time he had finished, having lost a couple of stones.

"You too can build a boat out of bird droppings!" was the initial reaction to Rod's attempts at welding for the first few days as the welding stick continually got stuck or he burnt a hole as he applied too much power. Eventually the shaking hand was controlled and some decent runs were achieved between the tacks he had already applied.

Richard organised the delivery of the steel and advised him to pay cash, "It's cheaper that way", he said. Richard was Rods mentor and although he never physically helped him his advice was invaluable. He lent him tools which he did not know existed.

"Go into my workshop" he invited, "You will find a 3 ton turfer to pull the steel round that template which is leaning up over there for the stern". This was without Rod asking for help but obviously looking helpless and in need of assistance.

Hawn Basin was a friendly community. It had a small clubhouse which was open any time a couple of members felt the need which was most of the time. Several parties were held whilst he was there and the accordion went down well at these events. On one occasion Rod had to be carried back to his boat after indulging in rather too much beer. The next morning two of the ladies who had assisted him commented.

"You were having us on last night!" and then explained. "We had no sooner put you to bed and closed your door when you leapt out. dashed into the bushes muttering," "Must have a piss".

Erick, his busking friend from Keighley, came to join him and help with a few labouring jobs and cleaning up after Rod something he was not very good at. When they had the energy they went out to find a pub to do a bit of music in and pass the hat round. On one of these evenings they came across a rather restauranty pub at which even Rod was not sure about asking if they could do a bit of music and pass the hat round.

"You do some of your 'Grappeli' style jazz and I will busk along with you" Rod suggested. They had tried to combine their styles on a previous occasion but without much success. Rod felt that they were making a credible duo and he was enjoying himself but after half an hour Eric put his flute down.

"Nobody is taking any notice of us" he said putting his flute down and refused to play on.

"Ok!" said Rod although he thought that they were being appreciated.

"Ill go round playing the accordion and you bring the hat", he said which was their usual finale.

"We wont get anything", Eric said refusing to collect. Rod went round stomping on the bass buttons with the hat in his right hand.

It was an almost record collection but Eric refused to take his half saying that it was his punishment for not having confidence in what they were doing. On the other hand it might have been that the customers were as tone deaf as Rod was and that Eric was right,

"But...", Rod thought, "...what the hell!" Eric was a slight figure with a self doubting complex to go with it. That visit was the last time Rod saw Eric. He phoned him a couple of times over the following years to see if he wanted to come on another canal trip but he had joined some cult.

"I am giving up everything to find out what I need", was his reason but Rod tried to persuade him otherwise.

"Eric!" he replied, "You have the wrong idea. You should be trying everything to find out what you want", but the advice fell on stony ground and he vanished into his chosen escapism.

With the hull nearing completion an engine was purchased from a farm near Haworth. It was an old tractor engine, a Perkins D3, and by pure chance it married up with the hydraulic gear box he had bought from a chap in Tarleton a couple of years before. After a bit more research he found out that it was the gearbox which Perkins fitted on their marinised D3. They ran the engine up on blocks to test it out and found that it ran perfectly. Eric was given the job of draining the engine oil and filling it up with new oil up to the mark on the dipstick.

A few weeks later with the steelwork completed, the cabin framework constructed, the engine mounted and stern gear in place she was launched without a leak!!
The time came to settle up the bills and fill up with diesel for the trip up to Yorkshire where he had booked a mooring for his boats above the five rise locks in Bingley. He and his estranged wife Belinda had been getting along so well that they had decided to 'give it another try'.

The diesel was the cheapest in the country but the electric bill was excessive.
"Why is it that your diesel is so cheap but your electric so expensive?" Rod asked John as they were leaving.
"The diesel is to encourage you to come here and the electric is to encourage you to bugger off!" He did just that with fond farewells and a promise to return. He had made some lasting friendships, Particularly John and his wife Brenda. She was not the easiest of people to get on with and seemed to be jealous of anybody who took up his time, which was everybody! She was a large strong looking woman who Rod and others found intimidating. George and the Dragon, Rod referred to them as which amused John but could not be relayed to Brenda.

There was Richard, of course, and Gill his significant other. She was a nurse and consequently worked shifts and could not always join in the club nights. Duggie and Audrey whose boat it was that Richard had built. Duggie was about 80 and had made his pile in South Africa but wanted to spend his retirement travelling the canals in England. He bragged about being a racist and said that even his Afrikaans friends thought his views were extreme. He was short, chubby and had a cheerful air about him. Rod used to just laugh at his racism which would have been funny if he could believe that anybody could be serious. He came straight out of a Tom Sharp novel. His boat was fitted out with anything ranging from donations to items from skips. It was very ecologically sound and much to the amusement of all who observed. He eventually named his boat 'Tramps Retreat' deciding against the name which other boaters had painted on it, 'The Price is Right'

There were probably 5 or 6 boats being worked on at any one time and it was the sort of place that either one of the men who was working, or one of their wives or girlfriends would come out with a tray full of mugs of tea. Usually it would be shouted out, "I'll make the tea!" and it would duly appear. On one occasion when the task had not been communicated, three trays appeared from different boats at the same time.

chapter seven

back to yorkshire

To help to crew the boats back to Yorkshire Rod enlisted the help of some old friends. Peter, an old lefty from the CND days came along with a young woman who seemed to snarl at life a bit like a bad tempered tiger. She was a 'women's lib-er', a staunch feminist, who Peter had rescued from an abusive childhood. Rod could imagine her leading a bunch of revolutionaries, machine gun in hand alongside Che Guevara. Peter, on the other hand, dressed more like a smart 'Ragged Trousered Philanthropist'. He hated 'muzak' which made it difficult to go out shopping as he would just walk out of any establishment with music playing in the background. Finding a pub without a juke box or muzak was even more difficult although he did love live music however bad it was.

One evening when they had just sat down in a quiet back room of a pub having just had the first sip of a much earned pint of drinkable beer and were starting to discuss the worlds problems and solutions to put things to right, the room was assaulted by muzak! Peter went up to the serving hatch and asked the landlord to turn it off. "Sorry!" he said, "It's all on the same loop around the pub" as his head vanished back into the bar. At this, Peter took a small pair of wire cutters out of his pocket and severed the wire leading to the speaker.

A couple of days into the journey the engine seized up on Crete so they had to tow her the rest of the way. It was hard work buttying her through the narrow locks but once they reached the wide canals it was easy.

It was out of season for the trip boats and, as usual, the Bridgewater canal around Manchester, which did not see many boat movements even in summer, was undisturbed. Rod almost lost concentration on steering as he watched the shoals of fish of all description passing under the boat as they proceeded. It reminded him of the River Air when he was a child before the millions of varieties of fish were wiped out in one day by some pollution from upstream of Shipley. The river had been covered with an endless cortège of dead and dying fish floating slowly down stream.
A few years later when passing over the same stretch of canal he looked in vain for a single fish. The same thing must have happened to this stretch and the canal was lifeless.

The last couple of days

he had to manage the boat single handed either because of the crew having to get back to work or just being too exhausted to cope with the early starts, the lunchtime and evening drinking and being told off by Rod for getting the locks wrong. At Esholt, the canal was too shallow to get the boats near enough to the operating side of the swing bridge to disembark. Rod tied the breasted up boats to the centre of the bridge so that when he opened it he could get back on and motor the boats through but try as he might it was not possible to get the stern of the boats near enough to get off and close the bridge.

"You should not be handling the boats single handed if you can't shut the bridge after you" an irate motorist shouted at him through his open car window. By this time there were several verticals whose drivers were getting impatient. Eventually, at Rods request, one of the drivers closed the bridge for him.

"Hang on a minute!" He said to the marriage guidance councillor who Bel had persuaded Rod and her to visit as she thought that it might help them to see things more clearly. This was after several weeks of him living back at the Hall and feeling that everything was going well. Their sex life was great and in between working on Crete he was back to doing jobs around the place.

The day before she had made the appointment he had been cutting out the apertures on Crete for the windows and in doing so had set fire to the welding cables inside the boat. It had been a bit of a stressful day.

Bel had been telling him that she did not think that it was a good idea for him to move back into the family home. They had both held separate meeting with this councillor and now it was a joint consultation so naturally Rod was hopeful that Marilyn, the councillor, would come up with some solutions to try and resolve Belinda's reservation about the reconciliation.

"Rod tells me that you are getting on better than you ever have done and that you have a fulfilling sex life?" Marilyn posed the question.

"Yes we have", our sex life is good!" Bel confirmed. "And we do get along well!"

"Don't you think you are giving him the wrong message then?" she said. This was the point at which Rod interjected with...

"Hang on a minute!" and continued with, "What are you trying to say?"

"Belinda has asked me to help you come to terms with the fact that she does not want you to move back in with her so that it seems that by having a good sex life she is giving you the wrong message".

"That's the first I have heard of that being the reason that we are here", Rod came back with in a confused tone of voice. "I thought that marriage guidance councillors were here to help couples resolve their differences!"

"Not always", she came back with.

Rod had heard enough and walked out. Life became intolerable after that and Bel reverted to the way she had been and one of the reasons he had left her in the first place. She refused his advances and virtually accused him of trying to rape her.

"Why are you being like this?" he begged the question knowing the answer but not seeing any logic in it. "Your previous actions spoke louder than words", he tried to reason with her. I've fallen in love with you again and am prepared to put things into the past"

"I can not live on a high peak of emotion. I want you to leave... Its too hard!"

A couple of weeks later after constant rejection and having rebuilt the engine on Crete he set off with both boats to Leeds. He had arranged with Pete, the lock keeper, a mooring for Crete where he could continue with the fit out and booked the dry dock for Waterwitch. Pete was one of natures gentlemen and had time for everybody. The school which he attended as a child overlooked the canal and he longed to work on the barges which constantly went past with their various cargoes. One day when probably only about 11 years old he jumped over the wall and on to one of the boats. He never went back to school but when the canal trade died he tried to get a job as a lock keeper. He was turned down because he was unable to read or write. Then, in his late twenties, he taught himself with some help to master this necessary art and had now been a lock keeper for some 30 years.

One evening after a long days work Pete asked him if he could run him in his car to an address a couple of miles away. Rod dropped him off at a terrace house on a dingy lit road in a very run down district. After about half an hour, with no explanation, he came out and they set off back to the lock house. On the way back they called in for a pint.
"Just a half for me", Pete said, "I can't drink since I had voiles disease".
"That's bad! How did that happen?" Rod asked.
"We were digging out the lock when the pound was drained a couple of years ago and my rubber glove was torn on a nail which scratched my hand", he explained. "I was in hospital for a couple of weeks and it's affected my health badly",

"That's a serious injury at work, you should claim compensation" Rod advised.
"British Waterways are in financial difficulties and I would not want to trouble them!" Pete said and would not listen to Rod's reasons for making a claim.
Not wanting to pry into Pete's personal affairs he had not asked him about where and why he had just been but Pete explained.
"I am on call as a Samaritan and trained to help with certain medical problems if no doctor or nurse is available. The old boy I went to see had had a mishap and needed assistance"
That was Pete, prepared to help anybody and not wanting to complain about anything. His death, a few years later, was due to complications resulting from the Voiles disease. The house went with the job so it was probable that his widow had to leave and was thrown out on to the street.

Two months further down the line the main part of the fit out was complete and Waterwitch had also been fitted with ice plating on the bows and waterline. For some time before taking the boats to Leeds Rod had been suffering from a trapped nerve which resulted in shooting pains down his arms. He had been to his doctor who booked him in for tests but in the meantime he had arranged have treatment from a Chiropractor in Leeds.
"I can treat it" said the practitioner after an examination which included an x-ray, "Its a trapped nerve in your neck but it will take about 12 weeks with three treatments a week and you could have to put up with it getting worse before it gets better". Rod agreed to two treatments a week for as long as he could afford it! In the meantime about halfway through the treatment the hospital

appointment came up. The results showed trapped nerves mainly in the right arm. The hospital doctor prescribed pain killers and said that if it got worse they would have to cut the nerve out of the arm. Just about at that time a report came out in the Lancet where they were publishing the results of the different treatments for that type of problem and the alternative treatment came out with the best long term results.

"How's things?" Rod asked Johnny, a boat painter of his acquaintance, when he came across him a few years later.
"Not too bad now" he said rolling his sleeve up and showing him a trail of stitch marks following an uncertain wavy path all the way down his arm.
"I had a trapped nerve in my arm and they had to take it out". "It was ok at first but I am getting the electric shocks again now". He reported. Rod told him of his experiences and that he thought the doctors had treated Johnnie's symptoms and not the cause. Johnny was in total denial and would not listen to Rods advice. He said that he would never go to a quack.

Volunteers for the journey ahead where easy to find. He almost felt as though he should be charging for the pleasure of narrow boating down to London. Louise, the archetypal unemployed single parent who was enjoying life with a bit of help from her parents and the odd cash job to supplement the dole, was renting the bunkhouse. She wanted to come with her three year old son but, unusually for her, she was working. Nevertheless as proxy in her place she allowed to go, or maybe was glad to see the back of, Ross, her Scottish medium built curly haired, alcoholic boyfriend.

"Have a good time, don't drink too much, keep an eye on him Rod". Were her final words as she waved them off from Leeds lock. Allen and a friend of his, Lydia came as friends but not a couple. They and several others in their circle were regular visitors to Thrushcross which was where Rod had become acquainted with them.
"Let me pick your brain?" Allen had always been asking, "I would love to live on a boat!" "What's it like?" It had been the same line of conversation from this man of medium build, medium intelligence, well dressed who appeared to have his life sorted out but in truth was far from it. Lydia was five foot nothing, stocky build, was some kind of civil servant and did have her life well sorted out. The forth member was Bertrand, a friend of a friend who would only come along if he could bring his motorbike with him. So with some difficulty it was strapped upright on the roof.
Graham who was the only one who had some experience at handling a boat took charge of Waterwitch with Bert and Ross as crew whilst Allen and Lydia crewed for Rod.
Lydia, who could hardly see over the roof of the boat, and Rod was sure, not past the motorbike, insisted on having a go at steering. Much to Rod's surprise she was a natural and seemed to have x-ray, kaleidoscope vision which enabled her to see over the roof and through the motorbike. A couple of hours or so down stream they stopped for lunch at a riverside pub with the intention of just having one drink before continuing. The beer was good the company was hilarious and the days boating came to an end. Ross was incapable of doing anything the following day after drinking himself into oblivion the night before. It was two days before he emerged from his sleeping bag.

The plan was to continue up the Trent from Keadby but on the last day the engine on Crete seized up again. Realizing that no more progress could be made until the engine had been rebuilt again the crew jumped ship except for Keith who had only joined them the day before and had said that he would stay and help with the repairs.

There was a small boat workshop next to the Barge Inn just before the lock. The owner was very helpful and lent Rod a block and tackle to lift and tilt the engine again so he could drop the sump and examine the bearings. The centre main bearing had overheated and nipped up so he cleaned it up and put new shells in. Three days later, with the engine ready to start and a new oil gauge installed, it was started up. There was a very worrying fluctuation on the oil pressure so another day was spent looking into the possible causes. Eventually Rod asked Keith who he had given the job of putting the new engine oil in up to the mark on the dipstick.
"How much oil did it take?" to which Keith replied.
"Up to the mark on the dipstick which took one of those measures!" he said pointing to a two pint jug. Rod took the dipstick out again and seeing that the oil was up to the mark he realised that it was the wrong one. A further gallon of oil was put in and all was well. He felt 'a right dipstick' as he realised that by asking lads who had no idea how much oil an engine might require he had caused himself to have to rebuild the engine twice.

Rod visited home to see his family. Colette was particularly pleased to see him and the fact that it would be he who was going to read the bedtime story to her because, with a ready made baby sitter, Bel was going out.

"Go to sleep!", he implored her as she emerged for the umpteenth time at 11.30pm. Crying and over tired she threw a paddy which was too much for him to take. "Right!", he said, "If you don't behave yourself and go to bed I will leave you to throw a wobbly by yourself". At that he walked out of the kitchen door and vanished into the darkness. He hid in the shadows where he could see the door and waited. It did not take long before he saw the door open and a plaintive voice called out.

"Come back Daddy", "I will behave myself". He tucked her into bed and she was quietly asleep within seconds. On her return, just as though the rejection which sent him away again had never happened, Bel took him to her bed and made love to him.

'Bloody women' he thought, 'But what the Hell. Enjoy it whist it's there'.

A week later and with a new crew of Louise with Tom and her brother Steve joining Keith and Rod they set off, in good spirits, again on the fast moving tide of the river Trent. He was almost sad to leave the two great pubs at Keadby but London beckoned.

"Can't you bugger off" an angry fisherman shouted at them when Waterwitch had gone aground on shallows above a lock on the River Soar. Rod was revving hard in reverse to try and dislodge her but to no avail so Crete was employed to try and pull her off at the same time as Waterwitch being hard in reverse.

"We would love to 'Bugger off'", they shouted back in unison. Another fisherman who was laughing his head off at their plight became almost hysterical with laughter at the added spectacle of Mr Angry dancing around with his swirling net, shouting abuse at them. It took them another half an hour to re-float after several of them had been knee deep in the water digging away in the blazing sunshine at the hard packed silt. By the time they had freed her the irate angler had packed up and gone.

"Best comedy I have seen for a long time", the remaining jolly spectator shouted at them as they departed leaving him to enjoy the idyllic setting with the pasture land behind him and the trees waving gently in the summer breeze on the opposite bank.

His crewing friends came and went as the leisurely progress saw the two boats heading steadily south. As they passed Berkhamstead they observed an irate woman shouting abuse at an unseen person inside a narrowboat which, as bystanders, they found highly amusing.

"And you fuck off as well!" She shouted at them which reduced them to tears of laughter..

chapter eight

rickmansworth

Rickmansworth seemed a good place to stop. There were lots of permanently moored boats above the lock and itinerant boats moored up below. Rod had met up with a few of them before and they seemed like a fun crowd to be moored up with.
Amongst the characters in this disparate group of people was a 20 year old called Dennis who smoked a lot of hash. He hung around the boats but seemed to have no place to sleep and just dossed on anybody's boat who would have him. There was a dodgy looking sallow faced individual who had just come out of jail. He lived on an old 72ft wooden workboat which was barely floating. He talked about his past mistakes and how his next job, a bank robbery, would be more carefully planned.

A gangly young girl who sprawled herself out in the sunshine in very strange poses looking as though she had very little control over her limbs. She lived on a small cruiser with a ramshackle wooden cabin which she must have built herself. There was Albert who described himself as a 'water tramp' and lived on the tarpaulin covered remains of a cruiser. He proudly told anybody who would listen that he had gone out to buy a packet of cigarettes 15 years ago and had never returned leaving his family to wonder what had happened to him. There was a young lad called Angus who went off to work early, dressed in a suit. He also lived on a wreck of a cruiser and was thought by the ex con to be an undercover cop.

Several narrowboats were occupied by retired couples who enjoyed continuously cruising the canals. There were a few other couples and individuals who lived on a variety of vessels, some of whom worked and some who signed on, getting the occasional cash jobs, smoked pot and got drunk. During the day Rod would work on finishing fitting out Crete and then join in with the barbecues and pub crawls in the evening. They would sit around a fire drinking the home made cider which a 'white van man' delivered in one gallon plastic bottles and sold at a price no self respecting 'alki' could refuse. It was a little cloudy but just about drinkable.
The conversation would range from solving the worlds problems, to where to get the best deals in cannabis, to the recidivist discussing his next job with a couple of other dodgy looking characters in open conversation so that everybody in the group could hear. It was a bit like being a fly on the wall.

"He's an undercover cop!", sallow face said on one occasion just after Angus had left.
"I don't think so", Rod said, not having any idea what one might look like and not seeing anything that an undercover cop might be interested in. The ramblings of Sallow face seemed more like a comedy plot out of 'St Trinians' or a 'Carry on' film and bound to fail at the first hurdle. There were no hard drugs in the group that he could see and the little bit of dope which was smoked seemed pretty harmless.

The moorings ran alongside a wooded park, where the merry band had their barbecues, with playing fields beyond. On occasions when their dole money had run out and the cheap cider had been finished, Rod would take a barrel of his home-brew along. After one of these nights he had staggered to bed and was immediately engulfed in sleep. He dreamt that he was having sex with a lass who he had been chatting to during the evening and in a half awake state realised that she was on top of him with his hands pinned back above his head. Before he became fully awake and still thinking that it was a wet dream, his hands were released and the figure vanished into the night. He got out of bed in a sleepy alcoholic state still not sure if he had been dreaming when he observed that the door was open. He locked the door, a bit late after the horse had bolted!, had a shower and went back to bed. The next day he knew that he had not been dreaming when a few of his, so called friends, made pointed jokes about some bloke or other being raped in the night.

On one of his trips north he had purchased a beautiful wooden yacht. It was copper bottomed, built in 1948 and had been a cancelled ministry of defence contract. The engine had been taken out by the previous owner to put in another boat so Rod had purchased an almost new DAF diesel engine which had only been run on a test bed.

During the ensuing weeks, along with the parties and the games of pool at the local pub, he was advertising both boats for sale. His intention was to sell them and go to sea in the yacht. He sold Waterwitch and rented out Crete to the homeless pot head Jim, on the basis that it was only very temporary until he had sold it.

"You realise that if Jim gets busted for dealing in drugs whilst he is on your boat that you will be implicated", Angus advised him on the quiet.

"I don't think he is" Rod said in denial of what he realised was probably correct. He also knew then that Angus was an under-cover cop.

He was just setting off north to commence the refit of the yacht at the time Angus advised him. He decided that it was highly unlikely to happen and ignored his advice.

On his return to Tarleton to work on Othello which was tied up against a much larger wooden yacht which was almost past restoration and was just a rotten hulk, he got in to conversation with a man standing on it.

"I am thinking of buying it" he told him, "I am looking for a project" To which Rod advised him not to touch it with a barge pole!

"This one is for sale", he told him, looking for a quick profit. Rod had only been there half a day and had only had time to lay his tools out for the job ahead. A price was discussed and the man went away saying that he would have a word with his wife. A couple of hours later he came back with a lower counter offer.

"No! I'm Sorry!", apologised Rod, "It's either my asking price or I am not selling". He was not really wanting to sell because he was looking forward to going to sea.
"Ok!" the man agreed, "We have a deal!" So, after only 48 hours Rod was heading south again to re-claim the occupancy of Crete.

Jim was not in the least perturbed at being thrown out after such a short time and with very little notice. Steve, the lad who had bought Kew from him a few years earlier, offered to crew for him up to Yorkshire, to get some hard boating done as a kind of work out to counter his sedentary office job.

chapter nine

the road to ruin

"Hi Babe, how about that drink you promised me?"
Why is it that everybody calls me Babe?" she enquired in a friendly manner whilst ordering him a drink.

At that point in time it baffled Rod as to why that particular endearment came to mind. It was not a word which he would normally use and in actual fact he could not remember ever having addressed anybody in that manner before. It could have been the baby faced nose which it turned out was the work of a plastic surgeon. Other people could have called her Babe because she never had a bottle out of her mouth but at this early stage in their acquaintance he could not have known that fact.

The beer was the one which had been offered in return for him carrying her recharged battery from the pub garage back to the narrowboat on which she lived. The favour had been asked of him whilst he and Steve had been tying up after a hard days boating. Rod found her captivating smile irresistible. She was a tall woman in her forties with enticing gypsy features, long black hair and brown eyes. The red glow at the end of her cigarette reflected in the whites of her eyes. He suspected that if this meeting became more than ships passing in the night that it would probably be the last drink that she would ever buy for him.

It had been a few months, not counting the odd nights with his nearly ex wife, since he had had a sex so he decided to go with the flow.
"I thought you were gay" she squeaked as his hands rolled her tights down over her firm buttocks.
"It seemed a safe bet to let you sleep with me" were her mutterings as she nibbled his ear and fumbled with his zip.
"Just because I'm a bit of an oldie with a handsome young lad crewing for me?" he observed, "You fooled yourself with that assumption, but, I must remember to use it intentionally sometime".
"Bastard!" she screamed as she thrust herself on to him with an almost instant orgasm.

He and Steve got off to a late start the next morning. Steve was none too pleased because the plan had been to spend a hard weeks boating from London to Leeds. That evening saw them at Leighton Buzzard for about 7pm. Rod jumped ship and legged it to the railway station where he caught a train to London to retrieve his car. It was 10pm by the time he got back to the Crystal Palace where they had stayed the night before. As he walked in to the bar Dusty was sitting on a bar stool with her drinking friends and nearly fell of it as she saw Rod enter the room. The round was on

him when her friends had finished deliberation about who had been right about some fellow or other, turning up again or not.
"I thought that I would never see you again" she whispered after they had moved to a quiet corner
"Like a bad penny" was his reply as their hands met each other's knees under the table.

The next morning on Rods return to the boat, Steve was as 'put out' as a jilted lover which made him wonder if Dusty's assessment about being gay might not have been half right. Louise, an old friend of Rod's, with her five year old son Tom and her alcoholic boyfriend Ross joined them again the following morning with the intention of crewing up to Leeds,

The night after that they moored up near Bugbrooke and found a very friendly local pub about a mile from the canal across fields, over stiles and through a farmyard. They took Rod's accordion and the bodhran along with Louise's tin whistle in the hope of a friendly reception and the chance to pass the hat round. Tom always enjoyed the music and, when the mood took him he was their star performer. He would dance wildly with his own cross between break dancing, tap dancing and imitating a whirling Derbyshire.

The small village they found was straight out of a TV soap with the pub being the social centre. It was early evening but quite busy. They asked the landlord if they could do a bit of music and pass the hat round. He looked at the disparate group who had just ordered a round of drinks with a certain disdain which all publicans seem to have mastered.

"Go on then", he grudgingly said, "But you'll get nowt' off this crowd". It went down quite well with it being a novelty so the beer money was secured for the evening. Rod played a few games of pool with the locals and then went back to join his band of revellers.

True to whoever had written the script for this soap a tearful girl whose boyfriend had been unfaithful to her was being consoled by Louise.
"You can have my engagement ring", she said to Louise at the same time as theatrically twisting it off her finger and pressing it unto Louise's hand.
"Don't be daft!" Louise said, "Take it back to the shop and cash it in", as she attempted to give it back to her.
"I will only throw it into the canal", she insisted pushing it into Louise's pocket.
Ross, who was not one to miss a trick joined in the consoling with a few drinks and kind words. By the time midnight and throwing out time came, Ross had completely taken over the errand of mercy and was last seen walking the girl back home. Steve, who had given up the idea of hard boating was by that time completely bemused with the events unfolding. The walk back to the boat was slow and the progress staggering as they took turns at carrying the accordion and the sleeping Tom.
"Do you trust Ross?" Steve asked Louise to which she replied
"It's not so much a matter of trusting him. The amount he has drunk he will be more than useless" Rod was not too sure and when Ross did not get back until after 4.30am he was even less sure. On the other hand his story about getting lost in the country lanes and not being able to find the boat could have been true.

Rod's mind was on other things, or rather, another person. He phoned her from Weedon; jumped ship again; a bus; a train and a car later, and he had collected Dusty. This was all too much for Steve who had come along for a marathon lock wheeling session and not as a voyeur of sexual canal fables. Before he departed Steve recalled the fact that after he had purchased his boat Kew, from Rod, he and his wife had been harangued by irate woman.
"They would..." he said, "...bang on the side of the boat and ask where a certain bastard called Rod was!"
Whist there could have been a certain mad woman called Celia who could have done that, Rod was sure that Steve was exaggerating and just playing to the audience.

Louise decided, when Rod had tuned the boat round and started heading south, that south was not her direction either, so after a couple of days when, they reached the point where she had been given the engagement ring, she tried to find the pub and return it, but failing to do so she decided to take her entourage home.

It was just Dusty and Rod on a slow boat to Berko. He had given her the usual line about being an eccentric millionaire and at the time after selling two boats and reducing his borrowings to a mere £5000 and having quite a bit of cash in hand he felt like one. He did admit that he could have been lying about one of the lines he was giving. Life with Dusty was like an everlasting boozy party. Wherever they were, the pubs seemed to have 'lock in's' until the early hour of the morning even if they had never had one before.
Their sex life was good as well. Brewers droop was still something which other men suffered from.

"My ex husband" she said, "Told me I was no good at blow jobs" she continued.
"Don't talk with your mouth full" Rod grunted fearing a Bobbit experience.
"I feel sorry for you men" she said after resurrecting his manhood to a usable state and achieving multiple orgasms on it. "You don't seem to be able to come again and again like we can!" she concluded.
'Multivitamins, where are you?' he thought.

They had been down at Berkhamsted for a few weeks and the end of October was fast approaching. This meant that the winter stoppages on the canals would be starting soon. If they wanted to get away from there and winter somewhere less pub oriented then they would have to start moving very soon. Dusty was not sure about the plan but Rod was certain that they must move.

The party was over, he felt, and it was costing him a fortune. They were in a pub every lunchtime, sleeping it off in the afternoon until tea time opening.
"A couple of drinks" she would say; then later when he tried to entice her to leave. "Don't be unsociable, David has just bought you a drink" It was nearly always a lock in until the early hours of the morning.
She did admit that she 'used to be an alcoholic' and asked him,
"Don't ever buy me spirits" He didn't, the Special brews went down fast enough. The fact was shouting at him but he had never had anything to do with alcoholics before, not at close quarters, not in a relationship and at that point it did not seem to matter. Even the fact that she had to take a couple of bottles of Special brew back to the boat with her after the lock inn's. They were not for drinking on

their return to the boat but for the next morning before the pubs opened.
'What the hell' he thought, 'she is a wonderful person and I love her. If I can get her away from here then things can change. I can help her'

They were living together on his boat. Her boat was the pits. Nothing worked on it except for one light which was wired directly to the battery. The porta-potty looked and smelt as though it had not been emptied for months. The shower tray was full of stinking unchanged cat litter. She had been extremely unhappy but now that they were feeling good together all the symbols of her despair were put right. The plans were made. They would set off the following day to spend the winter near some friends of his in Cheshire.

It was a party night. A going away party. A get as much booze down your throat as you can and kill yourself party. Dusty did drink a lot and then went on to the spirits. One minute the mood was sweet and light and the next; all hell broke loose. She hurled a torrent of abuse at him for not wanting to go on to another pub and stormed out saying that she was going to join some real friends. When he eventually found her, his appearance, was like a red rag to a bull.

This performance brought to mind the first time he had seen her. It had not registered before but he now remembered the incident earlier in the year when he had been boating south past the 'Crystal Palace'. It was the entertaining spectacle of a dishevelled woman storming out on to the back deck of a boat effing and blinding at an unseen figure inside the boat. This torrent of abuse only stopped momentarily when she noticed them passing by and laughing at her performance.

"You can fuck off as well!" she directed at them before continuing, with even more colourful language, the tirade at the poor unfortunate inside the boat.

"Remind me never to get involved with that one" Rod had said to the friends who were boating with him at the time.

That was she! This is her! The Babe from hell and here he was, with her.

'Not for long' he thought, and headed back to his boat to start the engine and boat like the wind to put as much distance between him and it before she noticed he was missing.

The next morning Dusty was all sweetness and light.

"It won't happen again" she pleaded, "I told you spirits were no good for me" They made love and all was calm and life was beautiful.

The only reason Rod was still there the next morning was because of a flat battery.

They started their epic journey in the early afternoon. It was exactly the kind of boating Steve would have liked. For several days they boated from dawn until well after dark. They did have a quick drink at lunchtime and a couple at night but never too much.

It was hard work. On the wide double locks on the Grand Union they breasted her small narrowboat up with Crete but when they reached the narrow canals they had to bow haul her boat through the locks separately. Her night vision seemed to be almost nil. He would throw her a rope in the dark and she would hold her arms out like a blind person. He would throw her the rope but if it missed her he had to pull it back and try again until she caught it.

"Too much sex!" Rod shouted to her as she missed catching it yet again.
"If it does make you blind then you should have a white stick!". "You!, give me too much sex!" "I should be so lucky" she retorted as her boat drifted away towards a weir which could be heard but not seen. "Chance would be a fine thing".
"Will you stop shouting about sex" came the voice of a figure in the shadows on the towpath. "You are upsetting my dog"

After they had rescued her little boat 'Alki' from the weir they tied up for the night and had a bath. They then went to sleep whilst attempting to make love.
"Mornings are my best time" she said whilst waking him up at first light.
"They are not mine" he replied at the same time as revelling in the erotic attentions she was giving him. "It knackers me for the rest of the day"
"Hard cheese" she said at the same time as laughing and farting up his nose as she positioned herself for a 69er.

It was the first Sunday in November and they had been boating from before dawn to get through a lock which was scheduled for a stoppage the following day. It was 10pm. And they still had two hours boating to do before they reached the lock which was to be rebuilt. A 'Navigation Inn' was sighted and was fallen into joyously for last orders. Fortunately they had not seen Dusty coming so there was no lock in. It was after 1am. before they went through the lock and tied up below it, exhausted, but satisfied at reaching their goal. When they arose late the next morning the work on the lock was well under way and all passage was stopped.

Dusty was divorced and had two sons who were at boarding school and an older daughter who was a nurse. She was only allowed to see her sons under supervision and was banned from visiting them at their school. Dusty had divorced her husband Brian because, as she claimed, he had been consistently unfaithful to her which had driven her to drink. In the divorce settlement she had been awarded a house and a small income. She had got into debt and sold the house to buy a cheaper one. When her money ran out again she sold that one and bought the boat. She had got seriously into debt again and in return for her ex husband paying off her debts he had cancelled her maintenance. When Rod met her it was some eight years after her divorce, she was unable to hold down a job and her mother was the only family member who spoke to her.

Rod's life was at a low ebb and seemed to be going nowhere. All that he wanted was a loving relationship. Someone to love and to be loved by; a friend, a lover and companion to share his life with. His estranged wife had told him that he expected too much out of a relationship and that he was too demanding and that he had more love to give than she could cope with and wished him, the best of luck, in finding someone who would come up to his expectations. Was Dusty, this once proud woman, who had been a female pioneer racing driver, the secretary of a squash club and a fully qualified dental nurse, was she the dawn of his long hoped for relationship? Was he being patronizing or even playing God by trying to help her to overcome her alcoholism. Was he in his early 50s still being a cock-eyed optimist? Time would only tell and for the moment the signs were good.

They had arranged to meet Rod's family at a 'Centreparc' where they were having a few days relaxation together. They were going as guest visitors for the day and arrived at the outer perimeter of this secure holiday complex at 8am. Only to be told by the security guard that the car park in the centre was full and that they would have to park there and walk the mile to the office where they had to check in. Rod protested at this and pointed out that they had presents to carry for his family who they were visiting. The uniform refused to listen even when he offered to bring the car back when they had unloaded the presents. Rod was furious so that when another car was let through the barrier he accelerated through after it.

The overgrown turd in the uniform brought the barrier down on to his car as he went through. The car had already been vandalized so apart from the roof rack disintegrating it did not do any noticeable damage.
'Oh God' he thought as memories of his impetuous actions had resulted in his ex wife not speaking to him for days.
"Sorry Babe" came forth from his lips whilst hardly daring to look at her as he observed out of the rear view mirror the diminishing figure of a man, brandishing bits of his roof rack, vanishing in the distance. It seemed as though his worst fears might be about to be realized as he became aware of the nearly speechless figure bouncing up and down on the seat next to him.
"I've always wanted to do that" she exclaimed as tears of laughter rolled down her face. There were lots of empty parking spaces for dozens of cars. It was the icebreaker; the topic of conversation with his family. That was after he had reported the outrageous behaviour of the security guard to the manager as he checked in at the office. The

guard was already in the office holding bits of the roof rack and reporting the incident. The manager apologised for the misunderstanding and as Rod left the office he could hear the manager shouting at the guard.

Most of the day was spent in the great tropical dome swimming, water chuting or just wallowing about in the Jacuzzi or just lounging around on sun beds chatting. It was late when they when they left the parc for their B&B which they had booked in a little village nearby. The visit had been so successful that they had arranged to join his family for a second day.

With some trepidation he drove up to the outer checkpoint the following morning. They had not booked and had not got a pass for the days visit so that the prospect of trying to explain this to the 'little Hitler' on the gate was daunting. Rod drove up with his window open but before he could say a word the guardian of the gate, with an almost look of terror on his face, stepped back and raised the barrier waving them through. He must have had a real roasting from the manager for the way he had treated them the previous morning. Rod did not bother going to the office so they enjoyed a free day at that Centreparc.

If money had not been a problem when his overdraft was £5000 it began to loom large in his consciousness when it reached £10000. Winter was upon them and apart from a bit of busking and signing on there was no sign of any work coming his way.
It amazed Rod how alcoholics gravitated, or, specific gravitated, together. They only had to be moored somewhere for a couple of days before they became

attached by the umbilical cord of alcohol similar to the one they had left behind in Berko.

Through his encouragement, over the winter, Dusty had regained her driving license, obtained compensation for wrongful dismissal from her last job and was taking action to regain access to her sons. She had not lost touch with them and they exchanged letters regularly unbeknown to their father. Rod's, then ten year old daughter, Colette, came boating with him several times a year and sometimes with his wife who always acted as though they were still an item. His two older daughters who were then in their mid twenties also joined him occasionally with their various boyfriends.

A phone call which Rod had with Dusty's ex husband when they were negotiating access to her sons disturbed him somewhat. There had been a note of utter desperation in his voice as he told Rod of dinner parties when Dusty had been blind drunk and aggressive. Of a school open day when she had turned up shouting and abusing everybody and had to be escorted off the premises by the police.
"The boys" he said "Had wet their beds for a month after that" and that it was then that he had obtained the court order restricting her access to the boys.

He told Rod of occasions when their daughter had to walk the young boys some two miles from her house in the middle of the night because she had been blind drunk and unconscious on the floor when they were staying the night in the early days after their divorce.
"No" Rod told him, "We both enjoy a drink in moderation" and that Dusty had learnt her lesson and that they were making a new life together. He told himself these things

but the night in Berko hung over his head like the sword of Damocles.

On their journey north both of Dusty's cats had jumped ship on separate occasions. She was quite philosophical about losing them.
"Cats are good at finding themselves homes" and continued "Let's get a puppy it will have a great life on the canals" This was not as easy as you might think. The RSPCA would not let them have one because they had no fixed address and neither would the animal rescue in Crewe where they were trying to give one a good home.

Crewe was one of the places where they went busking, or rather; he went busking whilst she went off to find a pub. Anyway, on one of her excursions just before she found a pub called the Railway Junction, she saw an advert in a shop window offering puppies for sale. Later that day they went to look at them. The mother was a long haired German Sheppard but they did not know what the father was!
"This is the last one" they told them, "it's the runt of the litter"
Despite the fact that it was over 8 weeks old she was tiny, pocket sized. They instantly fell in love with this small bundle of life and gave just a few quid for her.
"This is the dog food she has been weaned on" They said, giving them a small bag of dried dog food as they left.
"Let's call her Crew" Rod suggested, she is from Crewe and she is crew on the boat". It was agreed. Crew would not touch the dried dog food so they gave her a mixture of Weetabix, raw eggs and milk. She ate that as though she had never been fed before. Rod went out and bought her a large tin of Butchers Tripe mix which she loved. That tiny

little runt of a bitch, the dog, not Dusty, started to grow and grow as though she were being inflated. The biscuits she came with had to be thrown away because she would not touch them. It was no wonder that she was so small.

Rod could not put his finger on the actual moment when their relationship began to degenerate but it had a lot to do with him running out of money.
"No!" he would say, "We cannot afford to go out". She would go out anyway and somebody would buy her drinks. On other occasions they would go out for a drink which would escalate into two or three. He would go home and she would stay and scrounge drinks of anybody who would talk to her. When she returned to the boat it was his entire fault for not being sociable.

Spring came and things were getting worse. To cut down on the expense of pub drinks he would stock up with the really cheap strong larger from the supermarket as well as brewing his own beer. She would just drink everything in sight until it was all finished. He had to hide his purchases under the back seat of the car so that when she got desperate for a drink he would drive a short distance away, wait awhile then take a couple of cans in to the boat pretending that he had been to the shop a mile away to purchase them.

He stopped making the home brew, for all that he saw of it he might as well have siphoned it from the brewing bucket straight into her. Their relationship still had its good side so, he thought, 'whatever it takes to keep her happy'. They were happy in a kind of way and they both lived playing cards. Crib was one of their favorite games and it was great to challenge the locals in a pub where it was played.

To outsiders, alcoholics and couples in an alcoholic relationship can seem extremely funny and entertaining in a black humorous sort of way. It had become that sort or relationship with them. For instance-. It was spring and he had rebuilt the engine in her boat and was in the process of painting it. Both their mothers were staying with them for a few days. It was not planned that way but Rod had arranged to look after his mother whilst his sister and her husband, who where caring for her after a stroke, went on holiday.

"If your mother is coming to stay with us then mine is too!" Dusty insisted despite Rod protesting and saying that it would be best if they visited separately. Rod's mother, Dorothy, was delivered by his sister a couple of days before Dusty's mum arrived. Dot, as she was known, played on the inability to be able to use her right hand which she refused to exercise, and wanted everything doing for her. On the third morning, just before Dusty's mother was due to arrive she asked for help to have a shower. Dusty volunteered so Rod left her to it and went outside to continue painting her boat.
"That was terrible!" his mother complained as she came out of the boat afterwards. "The water was cold", she complained as Dusty apologized for not being able to get the hot water running.

That day was a success. The cold shower seemed to stimulate Dot into being more active and nowhere near as helpless as she had made out before. They met Dusty's mum at the station and visited the nearest town where they had a very pleasant day with the odd drink at lunchtime and then played cards in the evening.

The following morning it was a beautiful sunny day and Rod was up bright and early painting her boat. He then made coffee for everybody before continuing with the painting. The mums were up and about fairly early but Dusty stayed in bed until 11am. At 11.30 she emerged dressed to kill and announced that her and her mum were going out for a drink and was he and his mother going with them.
"Hang about!" Rod retorted, "Could we not have some lunch first and then go for a quickie before closing time" She would not consider waiting.
"Look!" He insisted. "I am painting your boat and I must complete these taped up panels before breaking off". "The least you could do in return is to make some lunch for us all".
She and her mum set off walking down to the pub about a mile away.
"If you go now" he shouted after her, "Then it is the end!"
"I have had enough" They went.

Dusty's mum was a nice, frail old lady, and on previous occasions when they had met, Rod had talked to her about Dusty's alcohol problem and she confided in him. "If I try to reprimand her and refuse to buy her drinks, she would not visit me"
It was sad but true and her mum was coping with the situation in the best way that she could.

When they returned from the pub in the late afternoon, Rod and his mum had just finished eating. Dusty ranted on about Rod not having cooked any food for them. Dusty and her mum cleared all her things of his boat. Crew walked out and vanished up the towpath. She was a sensitive dog and always got out of the way when there was any discord. The following morning Dusty brought Rod a coffee into the back cabin where he was sleeping and they made up. Soon after that his mother who was sleeping in the main bedroom brought him a coffee and found them in bed together.

Later that day all her things were moved back on to his boat after Rod had apologized. It seemed bizarre but after a while she had bullied him into thinking that it must be his fault, or, why would these things keep happening? Rods mother packed her bags and left whilst muttering something about someone being a terrible woman. He ran her to the railway station and she went home to look after herself. On her return from their holidays his sister was furious with him but it turned out that it stimulated a miraculous recovery in their mother's ability to be independent. Crew had adopted a couple of lads who were fishing a mile up the canal but she returned when all was quiet.

The drink was all consuming and Rod joked about being a trainee alcoholic. Heading for bankruptcy hardly seemed to matter. The one thing which he disliked about her was that when she had too much to drink she became violent and abusive. On an increasing numbers of these occasions he would walk out of a pub when she became aggressive and boat away leaving her boat abandoned. One of the worst aspects of these events was that she could not remember what had happened. They would make up and she swore that it would not happen again.

Dusty drove the car down to Audlem and said that she would walk back up the locks to help bring the boats down. Lock after lock went by but even with a bit of help from other boaters it was hard work taking Crete through a lock and then going back and bow hauling Alki after her. She did not turn up! All the way down the 18 locks. She did not bloody well turn up.

When he eventually arrived with mixed thoughts and worries about why she had not come to help but he found her in the pub with the local drunks.
"Where the hell have you been?" he demanded with rising anger to which she replied in an accusative manner.
"I walked up a few lock and asked a boat coming down if he had seen you" "He said that he had passed you moored up at the top of the locks past Market Drayton so I came back down to the pub thinking that you had not set off"
"You stupid woman!" he reproached her. "When he passed Crete you were still on her with me"
This exchange brought the house down and Rod was bought a couple of pints by the entertained onlookers. Dusty stayed in the pub whilst Rod went back to the boat and prepared a feast of roast lamb, potatoes, sprouts and carrots. In between his culinary efforts he nipped back to the pub for a drink. The food was ready for about 8.30pm so Rod went back to let her know that the food was ready.
"Come on Babe finish that drink and come and eat"
"Leave it till later, I am enjoying myself" she insisted.
"Come on! It will spoil" Rod insisted taking on the reverse roll. He left her there and went back to enjoy a much earned meal before going to bed absolutely shattered after the exertions of the day.

It must have been 1am when she stormed onto the boat and into the bedroom demanding why he had eaten without her and why he had not left anything.

"Its on a plate in the oven, just warm it up" he muttered whilst trying to continue sleeping. A couple of minutes later she was back saying that she could not find it. He dragged himself out of bed, went in to the galley, took the plate out of the oven and handed it to her. The next morning she took him a cup of coffee and expressed surprise that she had found herself sleeping on the couch.

The support group who help people who live with alcoholic partners was some help. He spent many a desperate half hour on the phone to them. The bottom line was that he had to put himself first and that sometimes the only way was to get out. He was out of there fast. Some friends of hers helped her to take her boat to Hawne basin. That was the end, he had had enough.

chapter ten

cannot sell here

He spent a couple of months in Audlem during which time he applied for and got another 'Enterprise allowance' to enable him to travel the canals painting and selling canalware from the boat as he traveled.

Rod's first inquiries for a licence to trade on the canals were made at British Waterways head office in Watford. They advised him to write to the Northwich office because his moorings were at Tarleton. This advice, He learnt subsequently, was incorrect because it should have been their Wigan office which would have been the correct administrative centre for Tarleton. His letter to Northwich explained that he wanted to travel the canal system painting boats and canal-ware at the same time as selling his services and craft work all over the country.

The letter which he received back was from the Apperly Bridge office confirming that a commercial license would be required. David Blackburn, from British Waterways, was the author of this letter, and he also asked for clarification and details of his proposed activities. This was replied to and a letter confirming the agreement eventually arrived in the post with the proviso that in the event of his turnover exceeding £27,500 pounds he would have to renegotiate the terms. The British Waterways management structure was, at that time, a complete mystery to him, so he did not question why, after writing to the Northwich office a reply came from Apperly Bridge. He realized, years later, that it should have been Wigan, whose region he was moored in, who should have negotiated the agreement. The only retrospective reason he could think of which could explain part of a mix-up was that his home address was in Keighley.

Wonderful!, wonderful!, absolutely marvellous, And a few deleted expletives thrown in to top up the excitement of the new venture ahead.
"No! No!" Said Watford after they had received his cheque for the commercial license, you need a hire and reward license, with a T on it, for trading.

He was just starting out on an Enterprise allowance scheme and money was not just tight it was fictitious, even the thousand pounds which he needed to get on to the Enterprise scheme was in the form of a letter from the bank, saying that he could have the loan. It was given on the basis that he could not draw on it. The hire boat license would have been about four times the cost of a commercial license. He wrote to Watford explaining that nobody came on to his boat, and that he just sold the canal-ware from the roof. He tried to explain that his practice was not dissimilar to the Coal man delivering coal from his boat. At the same time he asked what statutes or by-laws enabled them to insist on him having to purchase a hire and reward license for his proposed business.

Several weeks elapsed, during which time he had set off on his travels. When the license eventually arrived in the post it had a slip of paper attached to it apologizing for the delay. The foolscap sheet of the commercial license condition seem to be somewhat at variance with the agreement which he had negotiated, but, the fact that they had issued a license on the agreed terms was quite sufficient for him to feel secure and confident in his venture.

"Hi! Babe!" Came the sexy tones of Dusty on his car-phone which he had recently fitted into his boat.
"I haven't had a drink for two months. I finished with Burt after he beat me up. Can I come back to you please, pretty please?
Rod's heart sank, rose, rolled and froze all at the same time. On several previous occasions the relationship had not worked, or, should he say that the relationship had worked but that alcohol had destroyed it.
Her ex-husband had forgiven her once too often and had then engineered circumstances which led her to divorcing him.
They were childhood sweethearts and when they first met at school he was bottom of the class. The teacher's side-lined him as being thick and slow but she knew that he was not. She helped him with his school work and realized that he was dyslexic. A condition which was hardly recognized

in the 1950s. She helped him through all of his exams and after they had done their A Levels and he had got a college place, studying dentistry, they got married and moved to London. She qualified as a dental nurse. When she became pregnant and gave up work the dentist she had been working for gave her a glowing reference saying, amongst other things, that she probably knew more about dentistry than most dentists.

It is difficult to say at which point she became an alcoholic but It probably started when they were first in London and she would be left in the flat with not much to occupy her. She has given up the racing driving when a close friend of hers was killed in a race but she still enjoyed playing squash. He joined a dental practice in North London and they bought a house in the green suburbs. They were then able to afford an au pair for their three children which gave her the freedom to go out drinking. It was downhill all the way from there. She began to suspect that he was having an affair with a neighbour and with the au pair. She would get drunk and spoil just about any social gathering. He tried to help her to stop drinking but he eventually gave up and started taking steps to divorce her. She contested the fact that she was an alcoholic saying that her drinking habit could be controlled when it was necessary.

She sacked another au pair and then employed the ugliest one she could find. On arriving at a squash match one particular day she found that it had been cancelled and returned home to find, as she put it, her husband shagging the au pair on the bidet.
"It's not what you think" he protested as she stormed out thinking that it looked like an uncomfortable position. She divorced him!

It was not what she thought and if she had known that he knew that the squash match had been cancelled and that what she saw had been staged so that she would divorce him, she would probably not have divorced him, but she never did realize the truth. He did marry his next door neighbour after her husband had committed suicide on discovering that she was being unfaithful.

chapter eleven

again !

On many occasions, in his short relationship with Dusty, Rod had almost been driven to hitting her, but, had just walked away to torrents of unfounded drunken abuse from her. He thought that he had left her for the last time so what possessed him to set off and rekindle their relationship he will never know.

Hawne Basin seemed a long way from Audlem and in the normal course of events would have been two or three days boating. It must have been shear madness to have attempted to travel that distance in one-day and absolute insanity to have been getting back together with Dusty again..

A five o'clock in the morning start saw him at the top of Audlem locks in record single-handed time. The system of going into a lock, lifting a paddle, running down to shut the gate on the previous lock them running up past the rising boat to the lock above, lifting a paddle or opening the gates if the lock is empty. It is probably the best way of getting fit which is freely available to boaters. The boat is left ticking over in forward gear so that the bows push gently against the top gate as it rises. On the return sprint from closing the lower gate, a glance at the ascending narrow boat ascertains that it is not snagging on anything and that there is time to set the next lock. By the time the boat is returned to, it is quite often gently pushing the top gate open, and so on and so on, until you don't know whether you are running to open or close a gate or going up or down the locks.

Canal rage is a well-known phenomenon and the sometimes justified. On this occasion, after negotiating the flight of locks in the previously described way, he had decided, because of the slightly longer top pound to close the gate on leaving the penultimate lock rather than run down to it again. On approaching the top lock he was dismayed to see, as he went slowly under the obscuring Bridge that the paddle which he had a run up to lift was down and that the lock was filling up. By the time his boat had been secured in the bridge hole he was amazed and annoyed to find that the top gate had been opened and that a boat which had not been in sight when he had lifted the paddle, was about to enter the lock.
"WOAH!" he shouted. "Couldn't you see that a paddle had been lifted?" And continued. "Is it too much effort to just look under or over the bridge to see if a boat is coming?"...The feckless windless wally stammered,
" I'd just thought it had been left up."

"You should have looked" Rod shouted. And continued to lecture.

"You could have signalled to me to leave the top gate of the lower lock open, which, would have helped you and saved a needless waste of time and water."

Hyperactive probably described his condition at the time, probably hyperventilating as well after all the running and leaping about, so, after keeping them waiting, whilst he brewed a cup of tea and made some much-needed toast for nourishment, before letting them through the bridge, he felt a little calmer.

His Crew, the dog that is, just in case you thought that he was lying about being single handed, had slunk off down the towpath to get away from the raised voices. Later, she also sensed the return of peace and calm and was then sitting in her favourite position on the back deck and demolishing a golf ball.

There was no golf course nearby like there was when he and Dusty were moored near Sandbach, the previous winter. If she had found the odd golf ball then, it would have been all-right, but she found it much more fun to dash onto the golf course and take them out of play. Rod and Dusty did not realize that she was doing this until she went missing. They searched the towpath for a mile or two in either direction in case she had joined a fishermen, which she had done when she went missing before. Rod eventually went to the golf clubhouse to ask if they had seen her and was met with a certain amount of hostility.

"Oh!" It's your dog, is it?" "She's in the professionals storeroom under sentence of death,!" they informed him. She was so good natured that he could not imagine her attacking or biting anyone. They explained that they had been trying to capture her for the last few weeks, and, that spoiling someone's 'Handicap' was far worse than savaging them. The sentence was reprieved on condition that she was kept under control.

Canal-ware was not the first thing on his mind as he leapt around doing the locks, single-handed, but he did find time to put a few items on the roof. It was a long hard day and with no stops, except the enforced ones, waiting for Crete to rise or descend in the locks. These were the moments when tea would be brewed to drink with a sandwich which was hesitantly made at the same time as steering. The Wolverhampton flight of twenty three locks is a daunting prospect to tackle single-handed at any time and it was even more so on this occasion. Locks one and two were set against him and with their long pounds it was not possible to run ahead and set the next lock. The thought of the whole flight of locks stacked full, against him, brought about a despondent, resigned, feeling of the day's goal being impossible.

As he approached the next lock with its long pound the dread thought of having to tie up and empty it before entering, made him weak at the knees. Then he saw a figure winding the paddles up.
"A boat", he thought," Oh! Good, someone's coming down." But! It was even better than that.
 "Hello" said the lock keeper, "Are you single-handed.? There is a boat load of Americans about to come down", he explained and then cycled off to set a couple more locks for him. This was wonderful! Helpful was not the word for him. A saint would be a far better description. When they had passed the halfway mark the lock keeper cycled off to

see if anything was following him up. On his way back to set a couple more locks for him, he shouted.

" Leave the top gates open", and something about seeing where the Americans were.

Crete was about three-quarters of the way up the Wolverhampton flight when he saw the expected hire boat broadside across the next pound, trying, as novices often do, to get the boat in a lock sideways. It seemed to take them longer to negotiate the one lock than it had taken Rod and the lock keeper to rise up the rest of the flight to meet them. Then!, they irritated him even more by wanting to buy several expensive items of Canal-ware from him!!?.

With money in his pocket and the late summer sun still shining, the top lock closed behind him. The lock keeper seemed pleased with the painted mug which he gave him as a thank you, or, was he mistaken? Was his whimsical smile something to do with a play on the word mug? No! No! He was sure that it was not. He knew the lock keeper from several previous visits, Next time he would give him a teapot to go with his collection of mugs.

"I'm not going to get to Hawne basin tonight", he informed Dusty on the car phone. "Can you get to Windmill End for about eight thirty and we can have a meal at the Dry Dock pub. Dusk was falling as she met me at the far end of Netherton tunnel and the Dry Dock was as busy as usual but, unusually, it was candle lit. As he went up to the bar to order, much-needed, food and drink., The manager came up to him and declared.

"Rod! Do you still play the accordion?" And continued, "We have a power cut and if you would entertain until the power comes back on again there will be free drinks and food when we have caught up with the covers."

"Any other time," Rod thought as he wandered back to his boat for the accordion. Exhausted, knackered and, unusually, with enough money in his pocket to buy the food, he could not, in all fairness, refuse his request and agreed to the proposition.

The power came on eventually and the free drinks had been very much appreciated but the meal which they had been promised did not seem to be forthcoming.
Eventually he reminded their host about the food.
"The kitchen has finished,!" he said with a look of genuine horror on his face, that, in the turmoil of catching up he had forgotten all about them. At the same time as apologizing he dashed away to see what dish or dishes it was still possible to rustle up for them. He returned, with some success, and by that time they could have eaten anything. As Dusty mused the next morning.
"What did we eat last night?"
"Don't ask!" was Rod's reply, "Just don't ask!"

The following day he and Dusty took her small narrowboat in tow and headed off back to Cheshire. They spent several passionate days travelling only part of the distance which had taken him one days boating to be with her. They called in for a drink at the Talbot next to the canal at Market Drayton. There were several boat loads of young holidaymakers whose company they fell in with. After closing time the holiday makers invited them back to one of their hire boats. To give Dusty credit where it was due, she did say that it was probably not a good idea. They piled on to one of the hire-boats with the holiday revellers and someone put a can of strong lager into Rod's hand and a

tin of sweet cider into Dusty's. A small electric keyboard was produced by one of the lads who asked Rod if he could play it. This acted as some sort of catalyst for Dusty who had gone over her alcohol threshold.
"Will you stop making that revolting noise!", she shouted at him as she came through from another cabin, And then with a further, uncalled for, torrent of abuse.
"You bastard,! You fucking lousy bastard,!" she screamed at the same time as flailing her can of cider in his direction.
" Not again," he thought, felt and froze with the realization that she had gone over the limit." "There will be no reasoning with her!", but, still he tried.
"What's the matter now,? "he vainly enquired.
"You know what's the effing matter,! You are drinking my favourite lager and you've got them to give me this lousy can of cider."

Trying to reason with her was impossible, as also, was offering her the lager .She just carried on abusing him at the same time as pouring her favourite drink over him. That was enough! It took Rod only a few minutes to go back to his boat, start the engine, pull-out his mooring pins and head for Audlem locks were he wished, to hell, that he had stayed.

The following day he heard from his sister that his mother had been taken into hospital with another stroke. Just as he was about to leave the boat to go and visit her Dusty arrived asking him why he had left her stranded again. He had no time to argue with her and said that they must talk about things on his return.
Dot was in hospital and very depressed. The nurses said that she was refusing to eat so he tried chatting to her but to no avail.

"I just want to go!" she said, "I've had enough" He kissed her on the forehead and said that he would be back tomorrow.

That evening he tried phoning his car phone on the boat but it was not answered. He tried several times and in the early hours of the morning but it was still not answered. This was very worrying and his mind went into turmoil as to what that crazed alcoholic might be doing to his boat. He set off at about 4am and drove back. He found her in his bed with a guy called Barney. That was definitely the very last straw. He almost physically dragged them out, half asleep, and threw all her things out on to the towpath after them before boating off.

His mother died before he could get back to see her. He hated Dusty, he hated Belinda, he hated all women including his mother, they just caused too much pain. He left it up to his sister make the arrangements. At the funeral his cousin David said to him, Just remember all the nice times.
"I can not remember any", he replied, "She always criticised everything I did".
"Talk to yourself", he said, walking away.
Grief takes all sorts of pathways and he knew, deep down, that his mother had done the best she could but being cold and never cuddling him, putting him to bed at 6pm until he was seven years old when his father was demobbed, selling the violin he had bought without telling him when he was 13, wanting him still to give her money after he got married. These were the only things he could think of.
Grief can be hell!

chapter twelve

first blood !

It was becoming apparent to him, travelling the canals, whilst trying to sell craft work, that there were very few places where reliable sales could be made. The most successful ones were in busy tourist locations. With this in mind he headed across country to try his luck at Stoke Bruerne: After a failed attempt to sell his painted artefacts to the canal side shops in this picturesque little place, he continued with his direct marketing approach..

The moorings at Stoke Bruerne go all the way from the top lock to the southern mouth of the Blisworth tunnel, so, he moored about a hundred yards upstream from the shops where there was a space between lots of other visiting boats. Sales were quite good but on his second day, which also happened to be his third day of non-smoking, again, there was a waterways patrol officer who stopped and questioned him about his license. He told him that he had written permission, under the commercial license, to travel the country doing what he was doing it and that if he wanted confirmation of this he was to contact Watford.

The following day he was again sitting in the sunshine on the front deck painting coffee pots when the patrol person approached him in a very brusque and aggressive manner.
"I have checked with British Waterways at Watford and the Marsworth office and you do not have permission." He emphatically stated, and, before Rod could reply he continued.
"If you do not clear your roof immediately and take your 'for Sale' signs down I'll have to prosecute you"
"HANG ON!" Rod exclaimed, "You mustn't have spoken to the right people.".
Mr., Little Hitler would not listen! He just went on and on, very much like a drunken menopausal women. Rod should know, he had just got away from one.
"Go away!" Rod raised his voice at him."I have a living to earn and can do without you ranting on", and "NO! I will not clear the roof.".
He still went on and on and on until eventually Rod swore at him, told him to sod off, and went inside slamming the door behind him.
 After he had gone, and Rod had stopped shaking, the pub's takings went up by the price of a packet of fags. A letter to British Waterways complaining about harassment was also posted.

Trumped up little Hitler's in uniform always irritate him through their inability to enter into reasoned debate. On this occasion, because of his apparent recurring inability to sustain a relationship at the same time as trying to stop smoking, he just lost his cool, and to that extent, the debate. The museum shop and a little craft shop by the pub were the ones who had complained. This was made quite clear to him when he called on them again a couple of days later before boating on.

"It's people like you who make it impossible for shops like us to survive". Said the youngish women, in the little shop, with real vitriol.

"I am not going to even talk to you and would never buy anything from you, ever!". She concluded. She seemed to have no understanding of the real world and he tried to debate the merits of competition and free trade, but only managed to find out that shops like hers had an agreement with their local B.W manager, that they would have sole rights to sell canal-ware on that stretch of the canal. He knew that the canals were a kind of, time warp, but it now seemed that with regards to the law, particularly case law on restricting competition, they were in a complete world of their own.. A time when a garage was given a sole right sell petrol in that part of town and other similar restrictive practices were mainly a thing of the past.

The classic example of this which came to mind was the Wall's ice-cream case of the 1950s. Walls, a part of the Unilever group, tried to prevent ice cream vans from selling within a mile of their retail outlets. The matter went all the way up through the courts who found alternatively for and against them until it eventually reached the House of Lords. The Lords ruled that, in this case, there was no such thing as unfair competition and prevented Walls from imposing their embargo. Walls then subsequently flooded the streets with their own ice-cream vans. The result of this was that more ice-cream was sold and the price came down.

Backing down against the face of injustice is not part of Rod's persona so that when the summons eventually caught up with him via his home address, his automatic response was to fight the action. The normal not guilty response was sent to magistrates in Towcester and a long letter to the British Waterways asking them what game they thought they were playing when he clearly had a written agreement to do what he was doing. That action must have had some effect because after three adjourned hearings the action was eventually adjourned 'sine die' or as they say 'kicked into the long grass' never to reappear.

Winter on the canals is a time for contemplation, catching up with things and finding a good pub to moor up near, particularly during the festive season. Dusty phoned him occasionally, apologizing, and to say how much she loved him and missed Crew. Crew was the Alsatian cross, and God knows with what, Bitch they had acquired together in Crewe nearly a year before. She was now Rod's constant companion and a great asset when he felt like, or needed to do a bit of a busking with the accordion. His constant reply to Dusty's calls was an emphatic NO!

Eventually the memories of the bad times faded and transmuted into farcical almost humorous times. His fears were superseded by an overwhelming desire to be with her again. Dusty it was and not rusty. It dawned on him that he still had strong feelings for her. They were moored on the Cauldon canal and had taken stalls at several pre-Christmas craft fairs in the pottery towns.. They even did the odd car boot sale but the punters purchases barely covered the cost of the stalls. Every time they went out for a few drinks he was dreading the change from Jekyll to

Hyde and the inevitable happened on New year's Eve. They were at, Endon, a small place with two pubs. At least he could only remember the two which they went into. At the first one they were chatting to the group for local lads and lasses who discovered that Rod played the accordion.
"Go and get it!" They begged. "Is that all right with you, Babe?" He asked Dusty, knowing that somehow, quite often, whenever the infamous instrument was mixed with alcohol it could stir up a firmament of, almost, jealousy.
"Go for it!" she insisted. "Klingons on the starboard bow," she sang, to hoots of encouraging laughter from the warming revellers.
He went for it and had no sooner started than the, mine host, of that establishment asked him to put it away or leave.
"Come-on!. Let's go down the road", encouraged the crowd who had asked for it and half the people in that room left en-mass, all singing different songs to the tunes he was playing.

A couple of hundred yards is all that separated the pubs and as they crossed the canal bridge, Dusty suggested that he should collect the bodhran and tambourine so that she could join in. They were welcomed with open arms, like the Pied Piper who had collected half the village to fill the new landlords hostelry. It was still only about nine thirty in the evening when the crowd had made its unplanned change of allegiance and location. By 11pm, with a few breaks In the music, a couple of people in the back rooms requested that he go and play for them, in turn. As he went round the pub there were several young girls following him around playing his other instruments.

Dusty did not join in despite his pleadings with her on several occasions. The music was only a small part of the evening but during the intervals she would hardly speak to him and became somewhat distant. She even refused to let him buy her a drink. He tried to ignore the fact that she was deep in animated conversation with the bloke who was buying her drinks at the bar. Rod's drinks were on the house. By the early hours of the morning, and having, gone with the flow of the new year bonhomie, he was not expecting the tirade of abuse which she hurled at him with almost physical strength, as they, and the last stragglers were ushered out into the street.

In amongst the "Fs" and the "Cs", and other four letter words which he had not heard before, his comprehension of what she was saying, was on the lines off.
"Don't you speak to me like that again?"
"Like what?" he asked as she shot past him turning her head so that he would not miss a word of her venom..
"You know! You know!, Don't come that effing shit with me", were the last words he caught as he stood weakly in the black hole which was now swallowing him up.
When he arrived back at the boat, engulfed in the black hole which, for all the world, felt like trying to do a sack race in a bin liner made from wet carpet. It was impossible to calm her down. Even when he found out what she thought that he had said.
"You should be playing like this!", when he had actually said.
"Come on! You should be playing this!". Referring to the tambourine which a nymph of a teenage lass was enthusiastically wielding. And that, he was in no way

criticising her but only trying to encourage her to share in the fun.

She went on and on and at one-time, taking the cold dinner out of the oven, which she had hardly touched the night before, threw it at the low boat ceiling. The dinner, plate and all, stuck there for several seconds when, first the plate, then slowly a bit at a time the rest of the food fell on to the galley floor. Crew enjoyed the late snack when she returned to the boat in the early hours of the morning. At that particular time she was somewhere on the tow path trying to escape the wrath of Dusty. They laughed, for a few seconds, at the cascading spectacle and he felt himself relax thinking that the nightmare was over. No such luck! She started again. He could not walk out because she was on his boat. Her tiny little apology of a narrow boat was at the other side of the country so she could not be turfed out to paddy by herself.
"Right,!" he exclaimed in his much imitated way." I'm going to bed, I've had enough!". Despite all the trauma, sleep came instantly, but just as the peace of slumber came, it went suddenly, in a drowning dream, as a pan of cold water was thrown over him and he was woken to a verbal barrage of,
"You don't love me if you can say things like that". Again, the expletives have been deleted, for the sake clarity and to avoid too much repetition.
Frog marching her out of the bedroom and into the living area was about as near to violence as he got with her.
"Stay there!", he demanded, and don't disturb me again or you will be out on the towpath wailing to come in." he threatened at the same time as opening the door to let Crew in, who immediately turned tail and went out again.

'THUD', a heavy object landed on him and woke him up, yet again, from a few seconds of much needed sleep. As he staggered to consciousness he realized that his accordion had been thrown on to the bed,. The words of Dusty as she rapidly retreated through the loo door and into the galley were-
 "You think more of that thing than you do of me so you might as well sleep with it."

The time was approaching midday when he was awoken by her sweet tones offering him a cup of coffee and inquiring what he was doing sleeping with the accordion in a wet bed. The following day and in total agreement, they found a railway station where he bought her a one-way ticket to her mothers. Her reason was that she was not going to stay with someone who slept with his accordion. His reasons were less clear.

Rod continued on his travels meeting lots of interesting people. He still welcomed travelling companions some of whom joined in with a bit of busking and others who just went along for the enjoyment of boating. He met up with Pete, the perfectionist engineer, quite regularly. On one of these occasions Pete introduced him to a handsome looking woman of some 30 years, tall with long blond hair, who played guitar. Her name was Linda and she owned her own narrowboat and just travelled the canals taking occasional bar work.

It was not, love at first sight, but they bonded in a friendship with benefits. Greg, the musician, was at the event where they met and when he found that she was without an instrument and that, unusually, she played a 12

string guitar. He lent her a damaged one which Rod later repaired. She was fun to be with and enjoyed a pint as much as the next man. Her manner with people she did not like was cleverly cutting and could be abrasive but this was not a side of her which was ever directed at him. One pub they were having a very successful musical evening at, started to be destroyed by a few yobs who attempted to join in. They were fooling about banging the bodhran, the tambourines and triangle which they had taken out of Rods bag. He was about to pack up and call it a day when Linda started abusing them in the most colourful language. Rod was horrified and feared that they would get aggressive and vent it on him. They quickly, finished their drinks, put the instruments down and walked out.
"Feel sorry for you, mate!" one of them said as they departed, "Living with that!"

They were on the Ashton canal heading for Manchester and then on to Worsley. Rod began to see that Linda was not what she appeared to be. The sex was ok but he began to suspect that she had a history which she had not told him about. It was the amount of gel which she used before sex, it was some of the things which she said like,
"No man has given me an orgasm".
And on their first occasion of having sex.
"That looks a bit big!, I hope it will fit in!" Which he had found very funny and laughed at, taking it as a joke.
"I think that you have something to tell me? He posed the question and left as long a gap as it took her to answer.
"What?", "Do you think I'm a lesbian or a prostitute or something?" she eventually said.

"No!", but its not something I can say, it will have to come from you", he put it as tactfully as possible, still not 100% certain of his realisation.
"You know... don't you?" she eventually came back with. He nodded his head in affirmation.
"Well, I don't know what you're complaining about", she came back with in a defensive tone of voice.
"It's the dearest fuck you have ever had, It cost me £3000 pounds!" He laughed, not at her but very much at himself for the situation which he was in. He gave her a non judgemental hug and she, realising that the aggression which she had met with from a previous man, was not going to be repeated by Rod, began to laugh also. They talked for half the night. She told him about her childhood and the fact that she had been born as a hermaphrodite. Her parents thought that the child would stand a better chance of succeeding in life as a man so she went through several operations as a child to enhance the male organs.

As a man she felt out of place and began to realise more and more that her parents had made a bad mistake in registering her as a boy. She had tried her best to fit into the role of being a man. He was musical and had been in a pop group. He got married. He had a job as a telephone engineer. Eventually, in her mid twenties, she made the decision to have an operation to reverse those which had been done to her as a child and become what she had always known she was, a woman. After the sex change operation she went back to work as a woman only to get the sack. The Union, to their credit, fought her case for wrongful dismissal. The compensation which she was awarded bought her the boat and the lifestyle which she was now enjoying.

The following day they arrived at Worsley dry dock where they had booked both boats in to re-black the bottoms and replace the anodes.

"Derek has invited me out for a meal", she informed Rod a couple of days into their docking. "That's good", "Where is he taking us?" Rod inquired.

"Me", she said, "Not you! You don't mind, do you?" He did not mind. Her revelation had not done anything to enhance their relationship and although he considered himself to be broad minded he had to admit to himself that he was relived by the turn of events.

Her relationship with Derek blossomed and on being told by her a few days later that she was moving onto his boat, he was greatly pleased. Derek was, the salt of the earth, kind of bloke who had made his living on working boats on the canals most of his life. He must have had some kind of a ragged charm about him because even Marilyn had admitted, a few years before, that she had a one night stand with him.

"I really would not get involved with that one", Rod tried to advise him. "She has a terrible temper and is impossible to live with", he lied. It was not that Rod was jealous or wanted her in his life but, from what he knew of Derek, he felt that if or rather when he found out about her, he would not be able to cope with the knowledge.

"Have you told him?" he asked Linda. "No!" she said, "He has no need to know". Rod promised not to say anything. Derek thought that Rod trying to warn him off was just sour grapes.

chapter thirteen

may, queen, and i

The following year was spent reasonably trouble-free. Well... there was no real hassle from BW, only the odd grumbles from assorted shopkeepers and lock keepers. Women are always trouble, but, more of them later.

The selling circuit around the inland waterways was beginning to take shape. The Thames was good, particularly at Hampton Court moorings, during the International Flower Festival. Camden Lock in London, Gloucester, Devizes and many other places in the south of England proved very fruitful. The Basingstoke Canal was welcoming although it was winter when he visited it, so, apart from painting the odd pub signs not much business was done. The River Wey sold him an additional, ten pound trading license, which lasted for a couple of weeks and because it was the middle of winter they did not object to him using their moorings by the supermarket at Godalming.

The Thames Authority was a bit uncertain; in fact, they were almost schizophrenic in the various attitudes of lock keepers and officials to his, up front, signs and display on the roof. Their attitudes varied from.
"You can't do that!. Take those things down immediately or I'll have to stop your passage." To the other extreme of "OH! Those are great." "Can I buy a few mugs from you?"
A few phone calls to the Thames, Reading office established that they did not know the answer either, but, they would try and find out for him. A further few messages received and sent resulted in a long conversation with an Inspector Watts. He contemplated the possible use of their equivalent of a commercial carrying license, but decided that because the lock charges were based on tonnage, that the revenue from Rod's boat would be a pittance.
"The best way ahead," he said, "was to continue with the pleasure boat license". It seemed that there were no restrictions in their rules about its usage, providing he did not cause an obstruction or contravene any local by-laws in the places which he moored, they could have no objection to his activities.
"If anybody questions you about what you're doing, just mention my name" he concluded. So mentioning his name became the standard practice on the Thames after that, and, it always worked like magic.

Time concertinas and expands like rippling waves, or the distorted reflections in a funfair hall of mirrors. The mixed emotions of personal traumas and the contrast of the

everyday process of making a living gives your existence that very illusory feeling of being more of a spectator than a participant. Since separating from his wife and the subsequent divorce the old adage about.
"If a person is a middle aged and single, then, there must be something wrong with them". seemed to be proving very true.
The women who he had been involved with, whilst looking for the perfect partner, had either been just unlivable with, or alcoholic or neurotic control freaks. The latter were the worst because they could be like an over the top menopausal alcoholic but, without the booze, they could turn the terror on at any time.

In the summer following the final débâcle with Dusty and the skirmish with Linda he met a very pleasant lady, Viola was her name. She was gentle, soft, loving and a bit dreamy. Her work kept her, for most of the time, in the North of England, so, he set off on his travels, again, single-handed. During early summer they met up regularly. Vie would sometimes join him on the boat or they would go walking in the lakes or the Dales. Crew loved the walking; she also loved Vie, not only because of the walks but also because there were no raised voices. On one of her visits to his boat, they had just set off boating when Vie exclaimed in a quizzical tone.
"Rod! how is the boat moving?"
He was a bit stunned at this sudden interest, in the mechanics of the boat, so he started to try and explain everything from the engine to the gearbox, the reduction box, through to the propeller, but was cut short with.
"But it is not lit.!"

"What's not lit?" He asked her in a more confused tone than she had used when asking the original question.

"There is no smoke coming out of the chimney,!" she continued from just inside the boat with her hand on the back cabin stove, "And its cold, so! How is the boat moving?" She thought that the back cabin stove was the power source for the boat.

She had this sweet innocent curiosity about life which, if it had been possible to instil a bit more curiosity into her lovemaking, their relationship might have stood a better chance.

It was during that summer that he discovered the Hampton Court Flower Festival, purely by chance. It was the evening before the event started that he and Crew had moored up on the Hampton Court moorings. The main entrance to the flower festival was along the riverbank beyond the moorings. The whole of the following day was a frenzy of wrapping things up whilst trying, with very little success, to find the time to paint more stock.

"Why don't more people make and sell craft work from their boats?" Was a question often asked, then, before and since. They found it difficult to believe that, British Waterways, who control most of the inland waters, actively discourage selling from any travelling boats

"You don't know the, half of it," was often his reply, and, is followed by, "If you've got a few hours to spare I will tell you the story". This is what he Is trying to do now and the story would progress if women did not keep getting away, or, should he say 'in the way'.

Whilst it is a satisfying occupation to be painting objects with flowers and castles it is extremely elating to be selling them in large quantities. Most of his stock was sold in that one-day, so, that evening was spent painting, with increasing speed and reduced accuracy, more stock for the following day. There was no moon that night and by 10pm, when he took Crew for her constitutional it was almost pitch black. Suddenly the sky erupted into a blaze of light and explosions as a lavish, private fireworks display, for the Flower Show exhibitors, engulfed the sky. Crew, who was terrified of any air jarring bangs, ran off in all directions at the same time whist he was exposed reliving himself up against the elaborate wrought iron gates as other boat owners came out of their boats to watch the spectacular fireworks. He could not catch her, he could not see her or which direction she had taken.. She was gone.

After the display had finished he looked for the terrified dog until the early hours of the morning but to no avail. After a short nights fitful sleep, he dragged himself out of bed at five am. and set off boating, shouting and whistling, pleading for her to show herself on the bank. He boated downstream beyond Thames Ditton and upstream to Molesey lock where he secured the boat and walked upstream shouting for her.

The search for her was unsuccessful so he decided to return to the moorings, from which she had vanished, in the hope that she could retrace her footsteps. Another two hours were spent painting notices and fastening them to lamp posts and any other posts, offering a reward for her return. Phone calls were also made to the police and the RSPCA. Crew had his phone number on her collar, so, surely someone would find her and contact him.

"You're not supposed to trade from the visitor moorings", a not too unfriendly Hampton Court official explained. "You should contact Mr McGuinness to obtain permission". It was late morning so he explained about his missing dog and the fact that he had taken orders for several items which he had to paint for people to collect later in the day. He also promised that he would seek the permission of the operations manager.

Devastated hardly describes how he was feeling. It was a very long morning, so that, when the phone rang at about 1pm and a girl at the other end said.
"I think I have your dog", he could not have been more pleased if he had come up on the pools. The girl had a sweet Essex drawl.
"Is she all right," he asked and continued to babble about the fact that she was in season.
"Yes!" she replied, "I know that, I found her attached to my dog."
She thought that Crew was a lovely dog and had considered keeping her. They arranged to meet on the south side of Molesey bridge. He ran across leaving the boat unattended.
"Well!" He said after thanking her, and trying to persuade her to accept the reward which he had publicized for crew's return. If you will not accept the money how about going out for a meal.

The invitation was accepted and her Mother, who was staying with her, came too. The evening became magic, despite the combination which not only included Mum, but both dogs as well. Nearly all the pubs in that part of the country seemed to allow dogs into them. It was more like Cruft's than scruffs, with a dozy Afghans, lolloping Wolfhounds and cheeky Pekinese. May's dog Stanley was a handsome Brindle Lurcher, Crewe was Alsatian cross of indeterminate father lineage. May had found Crew about a mile above Molesey lock. This meant that his terrified dog had crossed a very busy main road and the bridge.

May was an early-morning jogger, and on that particular morning had observed crew sitting next to a fisherman. Stanley had stopped and taken an interest in Crew, but May had continued her run. On returning to find him, she had found them mating.
"Sorry!" she apologized to the fishermen. "My dog seems to be humping your   bitch."
"She's not my dog, she just adopted me a couple of hours ago", explained the fishermen. May took her home.
The evening flew by. They talked about living on the water which she had done once before, but on a houseboat. He taught her how to play crib, and, let her win. Afterwards they all went back to his boat to pick up a shopping bag which her mother had left there.

They were nearly there, when, the dogs decided that it was mating time again. They left mother to keep an eye on the dogs, whilst the two of them went for the bag.
The bag, Oh! The bag, it must have been planned. They fell into each other's arms, kissed cuddled and fondled.
"How about taking your mother home and then returning?" Rod suggested.   "Life is not as simple as that". Was her anticipated reply.
"It could be" was his counter. It was only talk; he knew there was not a chance. They returned to her mother, and when the dogs had separated, said a polite 'good night'.

Exhausted by a hard day's work, a night searching for his panic-stricken canine, and a stimulating evening out, sleep enveloped him like a wave of pleasant drowning.

Waking in confusion of the where, why and when, from half achieved, still dreaming pre-oblivion of deep sleep, can be very disorientating. To open the door of one's boat, in an undressed state and have a beautiful woman, some twenty years younger than you, fall into your arms in a passionate embrace is to be dreaming within a dream. It was not a dream, but the surreal start of a beautiful relationship.

The summer was wonderful. She would dress down to cope with the boating, and he would dress up, a bit, to try not to look too scruffy for his visits to her. The dogs enjoyed each other's company; Crew became very heavy with pups. They were born near Foxton. May was working so she missed the delivery. After five had been born Rod thought that she had finished so went for a much-needed pint of beer. When he returned there were seven. There were two white and black with bits of brown. They were like Dalmatians gone wrong. There were two, a bit like Stanley, brindle and brown with the odd white dots. There were two with a lot of white, some black and a little bit of brown. They looked a bit like Sheep dogs. There was only one which looked like Crew. The dogs had brought them together. The pups were their children. The world was magic through their love for each other, and the miracle of new life.

The living space in a 60 ft. narrow boat is quite large enough for one person. It is adequate for two people and two dogs. It can become a nightmare with nine dogs, particularly if seven of them are growing pups. The pups were containable but Stanley was not. He was not used to the boats and would chase anything that moved. Cats were his favourite quarry. He was bred for speed and strength.

On one occasion he darted down the towpath towards an unsuspecting cat. The cat attempted to jump on to his owners boat but missed and leapt into the canal, looking for all the world, like a cross between a spring loaded toy and a hairy kangaroo. By the time they reached the scene, the cats owner had rescued it, but, Stanley was trying to push the prone boat owner and cat rescuer, into the water with his clawing, clinging, feline fury. Whilst Rod pulled Stanley away and tried to apologise, all that May could say was,.

"There you are!" "Just what every man wants, a wet pussy!"

Stanley got his comeuppance not long after that. They were near Bishop's Stortford and the water was covered with a blanket of weed. He spied a cat and decided to walk on the weed. The look on his face, as he stepped off the back deck onto the green carpet, and slowly sank was worth seeing. His face was a picture that a thousand words of explanation could not describe.

It was a beautiful summer, but as they gradually found homes for the pups. May grew apart from him. They disagreed on politics, she seemed to prefer her negative equity, to the boating life, and she was embarrassed to introduce him to her younger friends. He did love her and he knew that she did love him; He knew!, but, women can be very pragmatic. They can switch on and off according to which direction their financial security appears to lie. Their lifestyles were incompatible, and neither of them was prepared to give theirs up. She went back to her ex boyfriend with the flashy car and the silly grin. Rod supposed that in his position, his grin would have been just as smug. She took the last of their puppies with her as a companion for Stanley. This fact was somehow comforting and to this day still gives him a strange satisfaction, to think that Ollie is still there, with her, by proxy for him.

For Rod's part, he went back to smoking and drinking far more than was good for him. Crew had to be spayed. It was too much for him to contemplate, the silly bitch, finding another heart-breaking partner for him.

On the third morning of that Hampton Court visit he set up the display on his roof with the few remaining bits of canal-ware after trying, in vain, to find the manager in order to obtain his permission. The morning was cut short by another visit from the previously encountered official.
"I have been told to ask you to leave or face prosecution for trading on Crown Property without permission", was his now, more severe approach, which was reminiscent of encounters with the dreaded B.W attitude.
"If you wish to sell your craft work here again, you should write to Mr. McGuinness and obtain his permission", was the more reconciliatory termination of his well delivered message. Rod, not too reluctantly, agreed to terminate his activities because, on one hand, he had almost nothing left to sell, and on the other, his Thames license expired that same day and he had just time to get to Teddington and down the tidal Thames to Brentford.

The following year a letter was sent to Mr McGuinness explaining exactly what he was doing and asking his permission to sell from the visitor moorings. No reply had been received by the time he arrived at the venue. When the patrol officer came round he explained that he had written, as suggested, but that it had not been replied to. On his advice Rod sought out this personage of authority. When he found him, he acknowledged that his letter had arrived, but, only just arrived.

"If your letter had not only just arrived I would have written to you to say no, but as you are here I will come on look at what you are doing," Mr. McGuinness said with half a smile in reply to his request.

It was on the second day of this five-day event when he came. Rod noticed him observing him and the public's reactions, from a distance, before he came and addressed him.

"I like your work so you can stay for the rest of the week," he said with almost enthusiasm, and concluded, " But! You must write in plenty of time before next years show to seek our permission."

Kissing him would have been a bit too much, so, shaking its hand with gratitude was as far as his thanks went. It was a very successful week and well worth the long distance travelled and for the cost of the Thames license

The Hampton Court venue was the most profitable one week event which he ever did. They were looking forward to the following year's visit.

The third years visit did not happen!. He wrote to the palace several months before the event but received a negative reply. It raised questions about his insurance, whether his Thames licensed enable him to sell from the boat, should he apply for local planning permission. They were also concerned about public access to the moorings.

His reply countered all the objections. Inspector Watts of the Thames was quoted, his public liability insurance was produced and he assured them that he only needed the Crown Properties permission, the same as they gave to the ice-cream vans, who were parked on the road above him, to sell from the moorings.
He was on his way down the Thames after a stressful time at the hands of British Waterways in Stratford before the letter from Mr. McGuinness arrived saying that they could not allow him to sell from the Hampton Court visitor moorings. He was devastated, but, he did not give in so easily. Several phone calls were made before he eventually spoke to the man himself.
His persuasive powers of debate! He felt sure, would win the day, particular because McGuinness had seemed so agreeable at their previous meeting.
"Do not bother writing or telephoning again", he reiterated, "There is no way that you will ever be allowed to sell from the moorings. It is against our policy."
This was his final answer despite the fact that Rod offered to pay the equivalent of a stall in the show in order to counter his argument that, apparently, some traders in the show objected to him. McGuinness had also suggested that Rod should take a stall in the show. He seemed to miss the point, that, the attraction of his outfit was that the canal-ware was being painted and sold from a narrowboat.

The Thames is a very pleasant river and there are plenty of places where one can moor up for a few days and sell a modest number of items in a leisurely manner. These places are perfect for hobby craftspeople but they were just fill-ins for those, like Rod, who try to make a living from their boat..

Their month on the Thames was of that more relaxed nature, Lechlade, Oxford, Windsor and several other places, where they spent time but with varying amounts of success. Windsor in particular could be very good. A fact which not many people are aware of is that the moorings on the left bank, going upstream above the bridge, are free-trade moorings, for about sixty yards between the bridge and the small slipway, after which are the trip-boat moorings. He had not seen proof of this, but several local inhabitants, over the years, had advised him.

"If you are asked to pay moorings fees here, 'don't'. They are 'free trade moorings' as defined in the 'Windsor Charter' and it's nice to see someone like you using them". Over the many times he visited these moorings he was never asked pay.

Henley Regatta had its moments, and one particular lady, had a rather wet dream, thanks to Crew. They were taking her out for a walk one evening after putting the roof away when the heavens opened up with a sudden and violent summer thunderstorm. Crew, who was chasing sticks into a little stream which feeds into the Thames, just above the moorings, was soaking wet even before the downpour. When the heavens, opened up, she shot off in the direction of their boat. She decided that a large white fibreglass gin palace was a nearer sanctuary. Not satisfied with just sheltering in the wheel house, she blundered straight through to the bows, and like a big, cold, wet 8 stoned, interactive mop, jumped into bed with a lady who was sleeping off a lunchtime excess.

The lady came out screaming and, Crew, who as we know does not like raised voices, had to be prised, quivering, from the double onslaught of thunder and a totally unnecessary raised voice, out of the damp bed. Despite their, entertainingly unconventional way of gate crashing the party, they were not offered a drink and had to take their lump of jelly on a lead reluctantly out into the, now diminishing storm, and back to Crete.
The 'they' at this time was Anne, but that's another story.

They did not visit Hampton Court that year but he was determined not to take the rejection lying down. A little research at a library helped him to draft the correct wording so that he could appeal to the executive. A petition to the Queen was eventually dispatched although it was not sent with any great hope of a positive result. That year was, after all, the Queen's Annus Horribilis. Rod included photographs of the boat and the canal-ware as well as an outline of the whole venture. Much to his surprise and delight he received a reply in from one of the Queen's Equerries thanking him for the petition and saying that he would be hearing from Hampton Court.

"Where is this horrible Rod Taylor, who's been writing to the Queen". Dennis McGuinness enquired of Anne, with as much humour as he could raise, when they checked in on the visitor moorings the following year with the permission of the Queen. The equivalent price of a small craft stand in the show was six hundred pounds. The takings were not as good that year as previously but it was worth it just win the battle. The following year they managed to negotiate a substantially smaller fee, on the basis that they thought their fee would go to the Royal Horticultural Society and that they would be able to avail themselves of the hospitality which is extended to the stall holders in the show.

Dusty kept phoning up occasionally and begging Rod to take her back. He was adamant that there was no future in their relationship. There were still several boxes of her belongings on Crete so he arranged to meet her and take them back. The meeting was arranged at a canal side pub near Uxbridge. The boat was moored next to the car park so he unloaded her belongings onto the back deck before going into the hostelry. It was still only about eleven thirty am. and the lounge bar was empty except for them sitting at opposite ends, of a table, away from the bar.
"Hi!" Babe" he greeted her, on approaching the table. Her face was black and blue with bruises. Her hand which held the shaking glass was also blue.
"Oh! Rod, don't unload the car." "Take me back with you", she pleaded.
"It's already unloaded" he confirmed and, "No way!". In reply to taking her back.
 "I'll swing for you yet!" exclaim Burt, addressing her as he downed his beer and started for the door.
"Let me buy you a drink", Rod offered, feeling more like an impartial observer of a farcical tragedy, in a theatre

production, in which he had once played the leading role. The world is a stage. This was a cameo of well practised actors. The round was purchased and Burt was again sitting at one end of the table with his back half to them with Dusty at the other end of the table
"I spent all fucking night in a cell because of this stupid bitch" Burt muttered into his beer, looking away from them and out of the window.
"There are some photographs I took at Christmas" Rod said, trying to change the subject. "They are of your lads and some of Crew, as well!" She took them, and looked at them in silence.
"Take me back" "Please!" "He'll kill me!" she pleaded. Burt downed his pint and stormed out.

Was it a set-piece? Rod mused as the distance, in time and credulity, widened with the increasing miles, as he came nearer to home. He heard, on the grapevine some time later, that when she returned to the boat all her artefacts had been thrown, by Burt, into a skip in the car-park. The last he heard of her they were still together and were well known for their regular performances.

chapter fourteen

barred, not bard

Stratford is the jewel in the crown of the inland waterway network. Bancroft Basin and the adjoining River Avon is one of the most scenic places in the country and despite the fact that thousands of tourists wander round almost all the time it still retains an air of tranquillity, particularly along the river bank. Bancroft Basin is under British Waterways control and the river is the Upper Avon Navigation Trust. (U.A.N.T) The chairman of U.A.N.T. is a most charming and encouraging old gentleman who, on first meeting, expressed an interest in encouraging craft boats to visit the river Avon. The BW manager, in whose region Stratford on Avon fell, was the most unapproachable, unaccommodating and unreasonable person Rod had ever, not done business with.

His first commercial visit to Stratford was up the Avon from Tewkesbury and it followed his first completion of the Kennet and Avon canal, A different Avon from the Worcester one which goes from Bath to Bristol, and subsequently, the Bristol Channel.

The K & A Canal Trust actually welcomed Rod mooring right outside their shop at Devizes.
"The more things that are happening on the canal," one senior member enthused, "the more people will visit it". This was exactly the argument which Rod was trying to put across to B.W and the small-minded shopkeepers who still could not see the possible greater gain which could be achieved through more attractions on the water.

The day before his booking to descend the Caen Hill locks, He was setting up the canal-ware on the roof of Crete, when he slipped. As he was falling, the thought was, "If I safely roll backwards, as I land, then no injury will ensue". The rounded top of the cast-iron mooring bollard which crashed into the back of his ribcage, proved the thought to be more than slightly erroneous.

Allen, a friend of his, who was moored alongside, came to his rescue. From the excruciating pain, it was obvious, that a hospital examination was needed. Devizes hospital is literally just round the corner from the moorings, which was the direction he set off in, with his help.

After a few yards, and with the pain increasing in exponential bounds, Allen had not stopped reminiscing about the various, of his, and other people's injuries. "For Fucks sake! Allen. Cant' you shut up and let me suffer in silence!" Was all that he could raise the strength to say. Two other people helped him the rest of the way to the emergency unit, whilst Allan went off in a huff at his rudeness, in the face of what he thought were his comforting words. He did kindly, put the roof display away for him and looked after Crew.

The hospital X-rayed Rod and kept him in because of blood traces in his urine. They said that they could not see any broken ribs on the X-ray which later proved to be incorrect. They had only scanned the main ribcage but not the lower rear side ribs, which it transpired later through X-rays at Airedale Hospital, were macerated.

By 6 am the following morning, stuffed with painkillers and anti inflammatory drugs he insisted that the booking down Caen Hill flight could not be missed. At 7 am they, reluctantly, let him out after ascertaining that there was no longer any trace of blood.

The only thing which Rod could do, down the flight, was to hold on to the tiller whilst Allan and his crew operated the locks. He moored up for a week at the Boat Inn, a couple of miles below the flight. A few whiskies made a good painkiller.

Devises was a place which he visited several times over the years he was doing the canal circuit. On one occasion he arrived there at the same time as Dave Dare with his pair of hotel boats 'Rose and Castle'.

They frequented an old pub in the square which was being temporarily managed by Peter and Jackie.

"Come and have a look at the cellar which we have discovered" Peter invited them one evening after several pints of scrumpy. Their host led the way down a steep ladder into the vaulted labyrinth followed by David and Mark. Rod went next going down facing forward instead of the safer way, backwards. His heel missed the rung and he went crashing down with his backside bouncing from on rung to another as he fell a full pint of cider in hand.

"That's the true mark of a professional drinker" Peter said "Fell all the way down the ladder and did not spill a drop" as Rod stayed sitting on the dusty floor taking a drink to recover from the shock of falling.

He became good friends with David, meeting up many times over the years at different locations all over the country. It was on another occasion a few years after that event when they were again on the Kennet and Avon canal that he and Anne decided to invite three couples, who had been very helpful to them, for a meal at the Cross Guns at Avoncliffe. The third couple was another David who was a boat owning dentist and his girlfriend Jeana.

They had been very sociable and had wined and dined Rod and Anne on a couple of occasions and David has been the 'knight in shinning armour' when he had picked Anne up from Devises and taken her to Bristol infirmary.

Anne had been following Rod on her little wooden narrowboat 'Annie Laura'. Rod had gone ahead on 'Crete' and had opened a swing bridge on their way up the K&A heading towards Caen Hill flight.

He had waited for much longer than it should have taken her to catch him up so he walked back only to find her doubled up in pain on the back deck. She had slipped and hurt her ribs.

"I told you to wear those non slip boots which I bought you!" he remonstrated at the same time as sympathising.

"But they are ugly boots, they would completely ruin my street cred if I were to be seen in them" she came back with.

"That would be far preferable to breaking your ribs in those flimsy fashion shoes" but it was too late, the damage was done. He insisted that she just sat down whilst he took her boat in tow. By the time they got just past the pub where he had laid up for a week with his broken ribs she was in very great pain. He phoned for an ambulance.

"Can we land next to the lock which you are just above?" the voice asked, from the helicopter which was hovering above them, over the car phone which he had in his boat.

"Yes!" said Rod signalling them to land.

"I am not going in an air ambulance" Anne objected "Its too embarrassing". She was taken to Devises hospital and virtually left on the doorstep.

"We no longer have an A&E here" they told her, "You will have to go to Bristol" Rod could do nothing. He was in the middle of nowhere and his car was in Bath. David came to the rescue and ran her to and back from the hospital, with a raft of pain killers and anti inflammatories, whilst Rod took the boats up to Devises single handed.

The date and time was fixed and they were expecting to have a very sociable evening with excellent company. It started to look a bit unsettling when they met up with The pub duo in the afternoon to take them the last few miles in Crete along the K&A to their destination when it became clear that Jacqui was drinking heavily.

Jeena arrived in tears saying the they had split up and that David had gone off with another woman. Dave Dare then arrived by himself because Cath had walked out on him.

"Lets make the best of it" Rod suggested as Jeena sobbed into her glass of wine and Jacqui was quaffing her third glass.

Except for Anne they all ordered steak which the farm owning pub was renowned for. Thick juicy steaks that covered the plat leaving hardly any room for the veg. The atmosphere was, to say the least, subdued and Jacqui sat there not touching her steak for some time.

"This steak is cold!" she said when she eventually dained to cut a small piece off and pass it through her lips. Rod asked the waitress if they could warm it up for her in a fruitless effort to placate the sozzled woman. When her plate came back she just pushed it away saying that she was no longer hungry. Not wanting to waste such a feast, Rod ate her steak and Peter took his wayward wIfe out and either went home or shot her for helping to ruin the evening. Either way they were never seen again.

Going back a bit to Rods broken ribs. Luckily the Nissan Bluebird which Rod owned at the time had power steering so that a trip to Yorkshire to attend his youngest daughter, Colette's, first piano competition was possible. That was when he ended up in hospital again, in so much pain that he could not move without groaning, and the broken ribs were eventually, discovered when Airedale hospital x rayed the back of his lower rib cage. After a few hours in hospital, and again, pumped with drugs, he discharged himself and got a friend to run him to Colette's performance in Leeds.

"I can not do it!" she nervously said as her turn came up to go on stage and perform her much practised piece just after Rod had arrived.

"You can do it!" the gathered family members encouraged her.

"No!, No!," I can't". she insisted.

"I am not driving over 200 miles with broken ribs to support you only to find that you are chickening out", Rod said, "You are being called", "Get up on that stage now!", he demanded. Reluctantly she went up on to the stage and performed. She won the first prize in the beginners section and subsequently told her dad how pleased she was that he had insisted on her doing her piece.
On his return, and with little help from Vie, who was back in his life again, he eventually reached Bath. The moorings on the river in Bath, just below Pulteney weir, and just by the side of the sport centre are free-trade moorings. The Brittas Empire look-alikes from the aforementioned centre go round and collect a fee of four pounds a night. A season ticket of twenty-three pounds can be obtained. Even better than that is the season ticket for boat club members of eleven pounds. It should be half the normal one, but, apparently, their computer cannot deal with fifty pences!

He spent a month there on the reduced rate, so it did not seem worth the hassle of taking the advice of some of the residents, who, advised him to refuse to pay, because they explained that they were free trade moorings. His time there was spent over the cusp of July and August. The weather was mainly good. During a first part of his time there Vie visited him a couple of times, but he started smoking again so, after that, she would have nothing to do with him. Sales were good although it was quite painful, at first, setting up the roof. The people there were very friendly and even a couple of shopkeepers, on their way home from work, would stop and chat about current state of tourism and sales trends in general.
"OH! It's lovely to see your work!" "What a wonderful boat!" was the general consensus, and again,

"Why don't more people do things like that from boats?" "What a wonderful life!".

Anne, who he had met during a short stay in Newbury, came to join him for a day to learn how to paint his style of leaves. It was supposed to be the canal painter's version of 'Come and see my etchings', but the invitation after a very pleasant day, of...
"Would you like to stay for the night?". Followed by. "Don't worry,! I'm quite safe with these broken ribs," was probably a bit off-putting.

The Bristol Channel was the only way back on to the canal system because the K & A was closed again, across the summit, because of a shortage of water. He set off with a chart, a compass, a mobile phone, a good anchor and crew consisting of his half cousin Simon an intrepid lady called Dee and Crew. They anchored at Portishead with the intention of setting off just before dawn, to go up the 'Shoots' at about four thirty am. With Crete, sitting quite happily on the mud, they had a few drinks and played cards until after midnight. Rod suggested that they draw lots to decide who should take the first watch, but, Simon said that he would not bother sleeping anyway, so, Rod went to bed and left them chatting. His instructions were quite clear, to wake him up at 4 am, or before that if there was any problem.

The sound of their engine woke him up, and by the time his boots had been put on and he had observed that the clock indicated it was only 2 am. they were well under way.

"The tide started coming in, so, I thought that we had better set off,"! Simon stated in a self congratulatory manner.
"IDIOT!" was the mildest of the words Rod can vaguely remember using. It was too late to turn back, they were virtually surfing up the shoots, two and a half hours ahead of schedule. He eased the throttle back as far as possible so that the boat could be kept under control. They could not see the leading lights ahead of them because they were blanked out by the arc lights on the pilings which were being sunk for the new Severn Bridge. It was a fifty fifty chance, they had to go either to the left or to the right of this rapidly approaching, blindly illuminating structure. Sod's law prevailed and the decision to take the starboard passage saw a ribbon of white water ahead of them. The tide was running too fast to take evasive action, in any case the bows stem was by far the strongest part of a narrowboat. Full throttle astern made no noticeable difference and they hit English Stones, which have sunk many a ship, at twelve or fourteen knots. The bows, momentarily, went up onto those partially covered rocks, then slid off again as the boat rapidly slued broadside and became pinned against them by the swiftly rising tide.

Simon, Dee and Crew who were inside the boat were badly shaken. Then, shortly after the impact, with the boat occasionally tilting as it was raised further onto the rocks. Simon came, gingerly down the gunwales with a rapidly cooling, half cup of tea.
" What the hell are you doing?" he asked as he saw Rod belatedly attempting to put a life jacket on.
"The captain is supposed to go down with the ship". Then Rod threw the jacket into the back cabin, not because of

what he had said but, being unable to put it on because he was shaking too much whilst holding on to the hatch sides. The only thing they could do was to wait. Whilst waiting Rod wondered who he could telephone, it never crossed his mind to call the lifeboat.. After several numbers on which he, not surprisingly, at that time in the morning, received no reply. One call which he made to a lady who he had been on chatting terms with, told him in no uncertain manner, where he could go, for waking her up at that time the night.

"That was no way to treat a man who could be about to drown!" he thought deciding not bother ever phoning her again. Not really daunted he phoned Anne.

"Hello!" Said a sleepy voice, "Who's that?"

"It's me; remember?" He reminded her that he said he would give her a ring sometime. "We are on the rocks, halfway up the Bristol channel, so I thought that I would give you a ring"

"That's nice! There's nothing wrong is there?". She said dreamily, but not in the least upset that he had woken her up.

"No!" he reassured her as the boat lurched at an acute angle as it was being pushed onto the rocks..

"I'm heading for Stratford, how about joining me for a day or two there." He invited.

"That would be nice!" came back the still sleepy voice, without a hint of sarcasm.

After pressing end, he wondered whether it was going to be the end but feeling that life was worth living, he again attempted to put the life jacket on just as Simon was coming down the gunwales again with another drink. This time it was a mixture of vodka, whisky and lemon juice. He said he had christened the drink 'Rod on the Rocks'. he threw the life jacket into the back cabin again after failing to put it on for the second time.

Just as quickly as they had been brought to a halt, they are away again. The leading lights were now visible as the illuminated monstrosity rapidly disappeared astern. They took the centre passage under the old suspension bridge and then hard to port again to for the western channel. They came near to disaster twice after that. Once, was bouncing past a giant buoy somewhere south of Berkeley power station when the, still rapidly rising tide, tried to drag them over yet more rocks.

Dawn had broken and the early morning mist, over the water, was clearing in the short time it took them to reach Sharpness. The entrance to the harbour is crescent shaped and a couple of hundred yards across. This is supposed to make it easier to enter the outer lock basin. He was aware of this and the fact that some boats have been swept out and up the river as the tide rushes through the pilings. Despite giving her, full throttle, they were being turned round in the swirling entrance eddy. With black smoke pouring from the exhaust as they just managed to make headway almost broadside on and as they entered the safe calm water of the basin the overheated engine cut-out. The crew jumped ship as soon as possible after that stimulating trip. Simon stays in touch but Dee has not spoken to either of them since.

At Tewkesbury Colette and Alice, a school friend of hers, joined them for the trip up the Avon. Colette was always curious about his escapades and asked him if he had another lady friend. He told her that he was going to meet a lovely lady in Stratford called Anne.

"Why are all your lady friends younger than you?" She asked, to which his reply was that if they were older than him they would be drawing their pension. Colette and Alice had gone back home before Anne arrived. When she did arrive they were totally at ease with each other. The couple at same table in the crowded restaurant they visited assumed that they were married.

"Have we been arguing?" Rod asked jokingly, for them to come to that conclusion.

"No!" Anne replied. "I haven't got the energy to waste time on activities like that!". Later as they sat under the trees by the river, enjoying the warmth of the summer evening Rod could not bring himself to make more of an advance than to gently snuggle closer to her as he sat on the grass below her. She made the first real move, which seems to be what women do. She casually ran her fingers through his hair and said how nice and soft it felt and then, without thinking, as though he was a child, started looking for nits,

"Women are always nit-picking" he commented as he took her into his arms. That was the start of a beautiful relationship.

chapter fifteen

flying testosterone

"You can't do that here,!" was the first thing he heard in Stratford." I pay a fortune to be able to run my ferry across this river." To which Rod's reply was,
"I have paid a double license fee to U.A.N.T. which allows me to do this." He went away, still grumbling, almost as if Rod was in direct competition with him.

That occurred on the river bank, opposite the Royal Shakespeare Theatre, where the moorings are partially shaded by the tall overhanging weeping willow trees. Both the river moorings and the Bancroft basin ones have a forty eight-hour limit on them. It is customary for boaters wanting to stay longer than two days, to alternate between the basin and the river. He had purchased a two-week license for the river, so his intention was to play musical boats between the moorings.

As he jumped off the boat with the ropes in Bancroft basin, Crew embarrassed him by leaping into one of the very ornate flower beds for the crap. Nobody seemed to notice because the plants were so tall. He could not tell her off because she was trained to do her business and a long grass as far away from the towpath as she could go. To her these, beautiful prize-winning flower beds, were just deep scrub.

On his first day in the basin he was bombarded by tourists buying items, chatting, and getting him to pose for photographs as he sat on the open front deck painting the various canal-ware items. It was not long before his second confrontation of the day. It was by the owner of the hire boat base which was on the river just across the road from the basin. He virtually accused Rod of stealing the bread out of his mouth. Rod sympathized, with him and told him about the time he had three refurbished boats for Sale in the late 1980s, and how the bottom had fallen out of the market during the property slump, and that instead of being a shipping magnate he was reduced to living on his one remaining boat, making a living by being a decorative tinker.
"My sympathies", he told him, "are with you, and, if I can do anything to help you, like handing out leaflets for your day and hire a boat business then please bring some round to me" He went away confused if not placated.

It was the B.W. lock keeper, or lenthsman, or whatever, who was sent down to put the fear of God into, who would not be placated. His message was to take his signs down and stop selling. The consequences, he intimated, would be unimaginable if he did not obey. It was the large hook which had replaced the lost hand which Rod found more frightening than their threatened legal consequences. Rod's explanation to him about his commercial license and the fact that he had the express permission of the Board to travel the waterways doing, his own thing, did not deter him from his delivery. To conclude the encounter, he sent his regards to the manager, and suggested that he came in person, to have a constructive talk about his visit. A repeat of the encounter happened every day he was in the basin. The sales were brilliant so that it seemed imperative to come to some arrangement with this, yet, unseen manager. A phone call was made to his office, suggesting that they met. A letter was also sent, suggesting that a civilized talk could resolve the impasse.

Towards the end of his second week of musical boats the rain fell continuously for two or three days. The river was in floods and not safe to be on, so, the basin was full of waiting boats. This suited him because, even in the rain, sales were better than on the river. With the daily threats from Captain Hook and no sign of the manager even being prepared to talk, he decided to move on, up the canal towards Birmingham.
He had it in his mind to visit Cath who was a well known canal character who was affectionately called 'Towpath Cath'. He had met her at a boat rally at Alvchurch which he had accidentally come across in his travels. As is the case with most of the small canal rallies, everybody knew each other, so that when the evening got underway in the marquee he felt a bit left out and after a couple of drinks went back to his boat with the intention of calling it a day.
'Sod it!" he thought and got dressed up in his busking costume with the hand knitted stripy leg warmers tail coat and top hat and went back in carrying his accordion.

It had the desired effect and the group of revelers who he had most fancied joining almost lept on him.

Cath was their center and the most outgoing bubbly person at the rally. By the end of the evening they had become intimate but on returning to her boat she had just passed out. Cider 'one', Rod 'Nil'. The following day he had to take Crew to the vet and Ann, another boater, offered to take them because her dog had an appointment. This particular Ann subsequently visited Hawn Basin and partnered up with John Rudge.

Anyway! Rod had promised to look Towpath Cath up, again, on his travels, They had met up once after that first unconsummated passionate encounter with a similar frustrating result so he set off up the Stratford canal to see if it was not, third time lucky.

Crete was an ex-station boat and was built at 7 ft 1 inch wide. One of the locks on the Stratford canal is slowly collapsing and is less than 7 ft wide so he had to turn back and go down to Stratford again. The rain had stopped but the river was still in flood so he had to spend another few days running the gauntlet of, an increased, twice daily harassment from B.W.

In his conversations with the B.W, office he ascertained that the main argument seemed to be that the council objected to travelling boats, like his, selling goods whilst moored in the basin. It was implied that he needed planning permission for his visits. A walk up to the council offices, and an informal chat with an official, established that the council could neither grant nor deny him permission. They had no jurisdiction over what happened on the water. The lady gave him a short, hand written note, to that effect. She also went on to say that, what the council objected to was the permanent ice cream boat and the proposed baguette boat taking up the visitor moorings. The visiting, canal related craft boats like Rod's, she assured him, were in keeping with the canals and welcome. The concluding proviso was that they would like to be informed by B.W. of these visits.

During the following year there was an exchange of correspondence between himself and Mr. Stumpf the, Stratford empowered, B.W. manager. Rod sent him a photocopy of the note from the council and also suggested that he would not mind paying a small mooring premium for a couple of weeks a year to stay and sell on the canal in Stratford. The response was negative, and at the same time as still, putting councils objections as the main reasons, concluded that he could not issue licenses on an ad hoc basis. He apologized for any inconvenience. His reply seemed unreasonable and after several more approaches, which he rejected, Rod decided that if he did not want to do things the easy way, that he would visit again the following year, as his national agreement enable him to do, and face out the opposition.

That first year in Stratford saw a new love come in to his life. Anne was easy to be with, not in the least judgemental and seemed to have a great sense of humour. Belinda had visited him to collect Colette and had stayed a couple of days.

"That's it!" he told her as she was leaving. "It's the last time we sleep together". And continued,

"You don't want me back, nor do you want to join in my lifestyle. You're just using me!" Her response to his outburst was one of slight surprise.

"I thought that you enjoyed our occasional reunions" was her quizzical reply.

"I do", was his answer, "but it has been a contributory factor in some of my recently failed relationships.
"Yes!" she said as she gave him a hug on her departure.
'She always was a deep one', Rod mused, and it was the way she said.
"Yes!" which made him wonder?
Crew, who was not sure whether to just sit on the bank, a couple of yards away with her pointed ears glued down, or, go for a long walk and find a quiet fishermen to sit next to. She eventually settled for the two yard, easy getaway, position.

That was it. He had made the final break with 'Bel'. If Anne would have him there could be nothing to spoil their relationship. He had started his life with a 'B', and then gone through the rest of the alphabet, so it would be good to find that "A" was the best, and that he should have started there in the first place. Dyslexia causes a lot of problems. The three cats which Anne brought to the boat, in two baskets, on her subsequent visits, found that crew was an easy target, by knocking the occasional artefacts from shelves as they leapt from surface to surface to keep themselves aloft and out of her way. They did not need to, because Crew was more of a scaredy-cat than they were. She would either hide in the bedroom, or go out onto the towpath.

As the summer drew to a close Anne seemed to be distancing herself from him. Autumn, and the stoppages, were fast approaching and he had not seen her for three weeks.
"Come down and see me in Newbury!" She invited.

Rod was moored at Sharpness waiting for a window in the weather before venturing back down the Bristol Channel again. He drove to Newbury that same afternoon and left Graham, who was crewing for him, to look after the boat and keep in touch with the harbour master. On previous visits to him, Anne had insisted on taking a couple of his shirts, back with her, to wash. When he arrived she was doing some of her own ironing and had just come across one of Rod's shirts.
"Damn!" "Damn!". "Damn!" She cursed as she whip lashed the shirt in mid-air, as though it was on fire and doing it in an attempt to put the flames out.
"I swore, blind, that I would never iron another man's shirt again!" She said with real feeling, and then, fortunately, joined in with his laughter, at her theatrical performance. It is one of her, really lovely characteristics she can laugh at her own, menopausal, outbursts;, most of the time.!?.

The phone rang at 4 am.
"We can lock out at 6 30 am." Graham relayed the lock keepers weather assessment.
"Sorry!!" he said to Anne. "Time and tide waits for no man!" As he jumped out of bed and got dressed.
The always say, ' that you can laugh a mature woman into bed,' but he was not sure of the significance of leaving her laughing, in bed, at four o'clock in the morning.

After an uneventful passage down the Bristol Channel and a couple more weeks in Bath, without a visit from Anne, he eventually arrived in Newbury.
"What are you doing here?" She asked with a note of sadness in a voice.

"I thought we liked each other's company", was Rod's somewhat, taken aback, reply.

"I do!" she replied. "But I don't want to get into a relationship!" she asserted.

When he tried with unassailable, male logic, to explain that he thought they were, in a relationship. She explained.

"When I spoke to people who knew you, on the canals, they said that you were, a main chancer!" and she continued, with a little prompting. "I was just using you as summers treat, and, thought that you would be away, with somebody else, by now!"

Rod's babbling s at this stunning revelation of hers, and her assessment of him, were probably a little incoherent, but she continued.

"You don't want to know me! I'm a disaster with two failed marriages, and, men are always trouble!"

"If!" she embroidered further, "I were a man, and knew what I know about women, I would have nothing to do with them, so, why do you want to get involved with me?!"

"You're lovely!" she concluded, "and you don't want to have anything to do with me".

"Your lovely too!" he said "I love you!, and stop bringing yourself down!" "I've, spent years going through a load of rubbish and now found the most perfect woman; I don't want to let you go".

"Look!". he concluded, "let's not call it a relationship or getting involved, let's just keep things as they are, and enjoy each other's company and the sex is ecstatic".
"Why throw all that away?"

"Oh!", "all right!" She said, as they fell into each other's arms again.

171

His visit to Stratford in nineteen ninety four was a similar story to the previous year. An agreement with David Hutchins, the chairman of U.A.N.T., a complaint from the ferry man and a visit from the hire boat chap, who took one look at him and stated,
"OH!" "It's you again." Then muttered something about complaining to B.W. as he walked away. There were regular visits from the B.W man on the ground, plenty of sales too, and praise from the public. By this time Anne was with him quite often and had taken up the painting in a serious way. Her roses and leaves were now better than his. That year his license renewal had come from the Wigan office with his moorings, correctly named, as Tarleton.

Andrew Stumpf was threatening to have his license stopped. Doug Picton the head Office license manager had written to him trying to explain that the commercial license was for carrying goods only, and not selling from the boat. He wrote back explaining that the written agreement, under the commercial license, did enable him to sell whilst travelling and that the agreement mention nothing about having to negotiate with every one of some, twenty managers, throughout the country, about where he could, and could not, stop and sell. In the meantime, Anne had noticed an article, in a waterways magazine, where Mr. Stumpf had been advertising for a craft boat to take a permanent mooring in Stratford.

Rod wrote to him and asked for details at the same time as expressing an interest in the mooring proposal. In the letter he explained that they would manage the moorings for visiting craft boats, as well as, using it themselves occasionally.

Stumpf replied that it would require some thought and that, his idea, was to have a permanent boat which was just a floating shop and could not be live on.
Rod's reply to that was that his idea was that it would be for visiting craft boats and that the only work which could be sold from them was that which had been mainly done on the boat, by the people who lived on the boat.

It seemed, more and more, that the people who worked for B.W., had no interest in the canals other than as a job and a business. They had a definite thing against anybody living on a boat and seemed horrified that the boats actually moved.   Moving boats could not be kept an eye on... Moving boat were an anathema to them, they could not control them. After that exchange of, ideas, they actually saw Mr. Stumpf on their annual visit to Stratford. It was in the middle of a glorious sunny day, with people thronging round the boat, when he appeared in shorts sandals and socks.
A lady was just asking,
"Are these things for sale?" Despite the fact that there was very large sign proclaimed the fact and price lists displayed in all the windows, people would still ask.
A voice from this spectacle of dress disaster interjected before Rod could answer.   "NO!", "These things are not for sale!" " He is not allowed to sell these things from here".
"Don't take any notice of him,", Rod interrupted. "They are for sale!" To which the interrupted person introduced himself.
"I am Andrew Stumpf, the Waterways manager". He now said addressing Rod at the same time as turning his back on the very astonished member of the public.

"You have written to me about coming to an arrangement about moorings".
"Yes, that's correct," Rod replied. He continued,
"I am asking you to clear your roof immediately. If you do not do so at then I will not even consider your request." was his ultimatum, "I do not do business with people who I do not get on with".
It was pretty obvious that, after three years of stonewalling, he was not going to consider any of Rod's proposals, so he replied,
"Surely, as a business man you will do business with someone who will not take any nonsense from anyone". And then paused for a second or two in order to receive, a slight acknowledgement of the assertion, before continuing.
"Well! Surely you can do business with me, because I am not going to take any nonsense from you! My signs will stay up; my display stays on the roof, because I have a written agreement which allows me to do this!".

They were two, middle aged, red-faced men in an angry confrontation. Rod in an effort to give him, what he considered to be a serious and narrow eyed stare in which he was sure that his eyebrows nearly met the bags under his eyes, whilst on his part Stumpf's nose twitched like an angry rabbit and the cleft in a middle divided leaving two tiny beacons of white light looking, for all the world like two illuminated zits. If there had ever been a chance of coming to arrangement with him, there was none whatsoever now. Andrew Stumpf was well known on the waterways for prosecuting people, at the drop of a hat, for minor breaches of the regulations. The fact that he had not done so to Rod despite all these threats, was probably because of the failed prosecution whilst trading at Stoke Bruerne. That matter had never really been resolved, so, sometime after the last adjourned hearing, he had written to the solicitors representing BW at Towcester asking them for an apology for wrongful prosecution.

The reply from Martin Kent Davies, quite clearly stated that he did have the consent of the Board, granted by David Blackburn, and that, in the absence of any variation, continues in force providing that he still had the appropriate license. It was probably because of this that during the following years attempts were made to refuse to issue the license. In the spring of, ninety five, when his license was due to expire, he had to telephone Watford asking them for his renewal notice. The notice arrived, three days before the end of February; when the license was due to expire. The remittance was sent by return post but the license took three months to arrive. He again phoned several times about it and was told that the delay was being caused by Mr Stumpf, who objected to his activities.

British Waterways were, obviously running, old-style, trading restrictions, on the canals which had been outlawed in our streets many years before. According to the shop owners, BW were charging the shops a premium for sole right to sell canal ware on a particular stretch of the canal. This must be illegal, because the canals are public highways by Act of Parliament, the same as any other solid public highway in the country. Just because B.W. have separate powers in the relevant Act of Parliament it does not put them above the law and case law precedent. BW's management seems to think that they are above the law, or they are so ignorant of the law that they just make up regulations regardless of whether they are contrary to it or not. In either case they should be woken up and brought into the real world.

It was on one of his later visits to Stratford when he spotted a narrowboat with some of Towpath Cath's friends on board. He was given the bad news that she had died a few moths before of Sclerosis of the Liver. She had lived life to the full and had drunk herself to death in her early thirties.

During 95 and ninety six, the Royal Mail was hot with letters going backwards and forwards, between himself, Mr. Stumpf, Mr. Picton the chairman Bernard Henderson and several others in whose hands his 'case' was put into, to try and stop his license. In various letters from Mr Stumpf he states quite clearly that it was a mistake for B.W. to have issued the agreement which he had with them. When Rod pointed out that, whilst they thought the agreement was a mistake, he was quite happy with it. It was pointed out to them that a renegotiation could be reached if they could offer him something better. Mr. Stumpf again after their eventual, reissuing of the license in ninety five, said that it had been a mistake to do so. He offered him, a trading license at no extra charge for that year which was in effect an agreement that he could sell things in the middle of nowhere, but not from places where there were people to buy the goods. This invitation was 'reluctantly', turned down.

In, ninety six, things, as the say, started to get really heavy. Skipton was where his boat had ended up for the winter. Anne was flat sitting her protected tenancy in London, because her landlord, Zukerman, was trying to get repossession on the grounds that she was living with Rod. They decided that the pair of them would make brilliant names for the two baddies in a novel. Zukerman and Stumpf.

License renewal time was coming up again and, as the year before, no renewal notice was sent on time, in fact no renewal notice was ever sent that year. Two days before the renewal date, he phoned head office, and renewed it by Visa over the phone. The payment was accepted, so, he breathed a sigh of relief.
"Too soon!" Too soon!" There came the cry, the battle was just beginning.

On about the fourth of March he received a phone call from Andrew Stumpf,
"Your license has expired and will not be renewed. You will now have to renegotiate the contract". He did not bother to enlighten him about the fact that it had been renewed over the phone but just told him in no uncertain terms, where he could stick his head. It did prove that his theory about them, trying to make him miss the renewal date, was correct. It also confirmed that they tacitly accepted the fact of the contract and would not dare to take any physical action to curtail his business. They were also, obviously, not going to risk the matter going to court.

The winter which he spent in Skipton enabled him to see a bit more of his family and gave him time to start writing. Anne visited him nearly every week for a couple of days at the weekend traveling all the way from Newbury. During the week he went to the regular folk evening at a local pub as well as joining a writers group at another. The friends which he made at these venues thought that Anne was a figment of his imagination because they never met her. They were to busy indulging in each others company to find the time to socialize when she visited him at the weekends.

He wrote a few poems and had one published. He started writing about his life and the more he wrote, the more he realized that his ex wife, Bel, had been two, three and four timing him in the early days of their marriage. He had learned some of the facts when people, mutual friends, some of whom were ex-lovers of hers, came out of the woodwork and felt that now they were divorced, they could tell him.
"It's all in the past, I can't remember!" was all that Bel would say when he tried to talk to her about the past.

All in the past, it might have been, but it was as though it was yesterday to Rod having only just realized the truth about what had been happening. The times when he had suspected her of being unfaithful and she had just made him feel as though he was being paranoid and made him feel guilty at doubting her. Eventually when he had tried on several occasions, unsuccessfully to get her to talk about the past, he received a letter from her apologizing.

>Dear Rod,
>   I would like to apologize to you for being involved with other people while we were married. I was young and had no idea about
>anything. I know this caused you a lot of distress and anger. Sometimes things only become clear in retrospect. I also wish that we had found & made time to do more things as a family and to do things as a couple on our own.

Next reincarnation hope to do better!
Love B

She also asked him to destroy the letter. It did make him feel a bit better but he was still angry. So many people, acquaintances, at that time knew what she was doing but did not tell him. He had been a, laughing stock, and could not help but resent it.

The middle of March was when the stoppages should have finished. Several boaters from the Skipton area had, like himself, booked in for the rally to commemorate the opening of the Armouries at Leeds. The new swing bridge which was being built at Riddlesden was not going to be finished on time for the boats to get to Leeds. All the other boaters receive notices that they were going to be craned out of the water and transported round the stoppage. Rod did not receive one so he phoned up to find out why.
"You are an unlicensed Boat" he was told, "and therefore do not qualify. And! not only that, if you do not remove your boat from the B.W. water it will be confiscated." It took a Faxed letter and several more phone calls to get them to agree that he had paid for the renewal.

The transportation was called off at the last minute and they were all told to meet at the stoppage in the, early hours of the morning, the day before the rally. There were about ten boats and by the time they had got through the stoppage they had only eight hours of daylight left to get to Leeds. The journey would normally take two or three days boating. Every swing bridge and every lock had a B.W. man operating them so they slid down to Leeds as though had been put on a pure silk sheet.

"The license..." Rod was now being told, "...is renewable annually and because of his refusal to comply with the chairman's request, not to trade within one mile of sensitive, areas; they were terminating his commercial license. His, counter-argument was that the contract clearly stated that in the event of his turnover exceeding twenty seven and a half thousand pounds he would have to enter into a separate trading agreement with B.W., implied that the agreement to renew his license continues until the terms are, mutually, renegotiated or that the stated turnover is exceeded.

None of their replies faced the question. They either skirted round it or completely ignored it. Rod's solicitor, Pauline, wrote several letters to B.W. on his behalf but it was still several months before his license was issued. The phrase she used was something on the lines of,
"I am sure that my client will abide by any reasonable requests that are made of the Board!" She was absolutely correct for but she failed to point out the obvious facts that they were making totally unreasonable requests of him.

Rod sent a letter, in the form of a survey, to all B.W. managers asking them where, if he were to ask, they would let him sell across the towpath, and what the reasons were for not allowing him to sell things in other locations. Two of them replied that in their areas there were no restrictions other than the normally accepted ones, of not causing an obstruction or stopping on lock moorings. Several replied just mentioning sensitive areas. Some quite clearly said that he could not sell within a mile of a land based shop, which was selling canal-ware. One manager sent a letter authorizing him to sell in, non-sensitive places. He wrote back thanking them for their replies, but, pointed out that their exclusion zones, for reasons of restricting competition, were illegal. The proposal which he sent them about setting up moorings, in busy places, for travelling crafts boats, received a cautious welcome. Generally the response was that it would need a lot of organizing.

On their boating travels he and Anne met up with lots of interesting people. One of them was the double of John Major. He liked his whisky so that he and Rod shared the pleasure on their occasional passing encounters. Peter was his name and he not only sounded like the Prime minister, he dressed and looked exactly like him. He had, apparently, retired and had always fancied a life on the canals. His wife had 'allowed' him to buy a narrowboat on the proviso that they would just live and travel in it for three years and then would sell it and go back to suburbia. They exchanged phone numbers but Rod lost Peters and never heard form him again.
Rod often wonders, on reflection, whether it was John Major taking time out, incognito.

chapter sixteen

rallying to the cause

After the Armouries rally they boated up to the opening of Tulle Lane lock on the Rochdale Canal. A short stay license for the Rochdale Canal was included in the rally package, so himself in Crete and Richard who he had just met, in his narrowboat Duke, decided to go over the summit and down to Littleborough.

The fishermen on the Rochdale Canal were the most aggressive anti boat lot they ever came across.
"You are going too fast," was the constant cry, even when the boats were hardly moving. They threw bait at them and at one lock Rod's propeller picked up, what can only be described as, a very well designed propeller stopper. It was like a giant rag mop head of over a yard in diameter. It was made up of a mixture of a fabric strips nylon thread, reinforced package casing binding and many other wiry, stringy things. It took four hours to cut it off the propeller.

It was definitely a man-made object designed specially to foul up a propeller.

The fishermen had made up a rule that, boats could only move from 8am to 4pm. The Rochdale Canal Society, boating members, told them to ignore the restriction so, having been held up for half the day by a fisherman's invention, they had to boat on into the evening to make up the lost time.

The Rochdale canal has the highest summit without a tunnel, and, like many other canals it has lost its feeder reservoir to farmers for irrigation. On their way up to the summit they had some difficulties with lock gates and paddle gear, but, the first part of the descent on the other side was real pioneering stuff.

Although the first few gates had been replaced in recent years, the locks had been left empty and the pounds very low so the gates were more like vertical waterfalls when they attempted to fill them. The third lock down had become too narrow to get both boats in, so they decided to leave 'Crete' in the pound above and go to Littleborough with Richard on his boat, Duke. The first few locks were also full of rocks and debris, some of which they had to clear, in order to operate the gates. It was obvious that they were the first boats down since the reopening. The locks after that were used by the odd trip boats and a few of the other craft, which resided on that, once isolated, section. As they were approaching the boat yard, a mile or two, from the current end of the canal, they noticed a flurry of activity. The workers in the boatyard signalled them to, moor up, making them wonder what we had done wrong. They were as excited as natives on a tropical island who were seeing white men for the first time.

"Where are all the other boats which we were expecting?" They asked, handing them special certificates for the first boats over the summit in fifty years. They told them of their difficulties and, of the now shortage of water on the summit.

Two small narrow boats passed them in the outward direction, as they were on their way back after a pint of beer in the pub at the end of the navigation.

It was dark when they reached Crete again which was now sitting on the mud in the, fast emptying, pound. The next morning it took nearly an hour to let enough water down to float 'Crete', and by the time they had reached the summit the level there was looking very low. Crete is nearly three foot draft and they only just made it across the top. The two smaller narrow boats which had yet to return, were more modern, and only about eighteen inches draft, so they managed the return also, but, the top pound was closed after that until further rain.

Richard in his narrowboat Duke had a very short term memory which was the result of serious head injuries. During conversations with him it turned out that he was a convicted pedophile and that the injuries had been inflicted by a mob to encourage him to leave his house in the estate where he lived which was why he was living on a boat.

On the way down the locks through Todmorden Richards windless slipped on one of the very stiff winding gears and flew round hitting him on the head and knocked him unconscious. An ambulance had to be called and he was taken off to hospital. Rod continued to take the boats

down, breasted up, single handed until Richard was discharged the following day.
"It's just God punishing me again for my condition" he said, philosophically on his return.

As the year progressed Rod attended more rallies than he had ever done before. The Nottingham Boat show was next which turned out to be the last of that event. To get free tickets he entered the regional heat of the Royal Yacht Associations Volvo Penta boat handling competition. At the last minute the cooling system on Crete developed a leak. BW lent him their centre cockpit cruiser. Despite having never handled a boat like that before, and also doing it single-handed, because he did not know that the event allowed as many crew as the captain wanted, he came first and qualified for the finals in Southampton later that summer.

The competition involved several manoeuvres one of which was rescuing a drifting vessel. He positioned the boat bow to bow with the drifting boat and climbed out of the wheelhouse to catch a rope from the crew of the drifter. On climbing out he realised that his boat was still in gear so he momentarily stopped with intention of going back in and knocking it out of gear. He realised that the mistake was keeping the boats close together in a tight slow circle so he proceeded to tie the other boat on and then take her to the landing pontoon as was required. As well as the judges on the bank there was one on board the boat to observe, at close quarters, its handling. The final manoeuvre was a timed circuit and as he was coming in on the home stretch there was a trip boat heading towards him at a distance which he calculated he could just get to the landing stage without hindering its passage. As he went in he realised that the trip boat was going faster than he had calculated and had to accelerate. It was near disaster as he headed almost bow first towards the pontoon at speed. Reversing at that trajectory would have sent him head on into the pontoon so he threw the wheel hard over to port, gave the throttle a short blast in forward bringing the boat parallel with landing stage before slamming it into reverse. His boat stopped bang on target and he jumped off and tied her up as though the whole handling had been planned.

"He really knows how to handle a boat" Anne overheard one of the judges comment to another as he completed the course. Little did they know!

The final was to be in Southampton later that year, in a quarter of a million pound boat, so he was looking forward to that.

Braunston boat show was next on the list. It is one of the best narrowboat rallies and although sales were not brilliant it was a most enjoyable event. He then boated down the Grand Union and on to the Thames for Hampton Court flower show, Henley Regatta and several other good venues to sell canal-ware on this royal river.

The K.& A. canal then beckoned him and after a stay in Devizes and Bath, the now familiar, Bristol Channel loomed large ahead of them. There have been a few, uneventful trips on this notorious stretch of water but not on this occasion. They dragged anchor, in the middle of the night as the tide was still going out. They were being swept swiftly over the rocks beyond Portishead pier. It was a panic situation so the crew was awoken as Rod started the engine whilst they, Clive and John, were on the front deck attempting to retrieve the anchor. They gave him hand signals, as to which direction to go, in order to gain slack to pull in the chain and snatch the anchor from a holding position. In the pitch black moonless night they could hardly see anything but the loud sound of rushing water over rocks meant that we were very close to disaster.

On the front deck, unseen by Rod whilst Clive and John were taking in the anchor, Anne was leaning over the cratch front holding onto them to help them keep their balance. 'Crew', at this point, decided that she wanted to join in and climbed on top of them all. Unheard, by Rod, were their cursing of the captain and his uncontrollable dog. They just managed to make sufficient headway to beach Crete higher up on the mud on the safe side of the pier. After the tide had turned they waited for the correct window in the rising tide to enable them to have a safe journey up to Sharpness. Jan and Richard slept on unperturbed by the sounds of the frantic survival activities which were being played out before and aft of them. If he had a belief in witchcraft Rod might have thought that a certain Mr. Stumpf could have had a hand in the Bristol Channel events.

chapter seventeen

stratford again!

Gloucester docks with its original eighteenth and nineteenth century warehousing does evoke an image of another age. Most of these monolithic buildings have been put to new uses but a couple of them were still in their original but, unused state. B.W. have offices and a museum and one of the warehouses. They tried to sell their canal-ware to the museum shop but their prices were far too expensive for them and, by the time they had put their mark-up on it would have made the price of theirs twice that of comparable pieces. Most of the work in the shops is very peremptory. It is produced at such a speed that any feeling of pleasure either in the execution or, in Rod and Annie's opinion, for the beholder is lost. They put twice the care into their work which is why, when people are given a choice, they purchase theirs..

They did not have any harassment whilst selling from the boat in the docks. On one occasion a B.W. person did comment that they should, probably, not be selling the things, but she shrugged her shoulders, and said that she thought the work was nice and then walked away.

On their way up to Stratford that year Rod began to experience opposition from U.A.N.T. David Hutchins was very apologetic, but he told Rod that Stratford district council had threatened that if he allowed boats to sell craft work from the park moorings they would ban all boats from mooring there. This was an astonishing turnaround, so on his way up the river he phoned the council and arranged an on-site meeting. At the meeting it was agreed, that because, U.A.N.T. had already given him permission that his 'activities' it would be allowed for that visit.

This was beginning to become utterly ridiculous. Anybody would think that he was selling drugs or running a floating brothel rather than trying to make an honest living and a very meagre living, to boot, painting and selling canal-ware from the narrowboat. The incongruity, if there is any, is that selling canal-ware from a land-based shop is ok but not selling it from a 'bloody' boat! He mused angrily to himself.

A further approach to the council and some research by a lady in one of the departments, the architects or the planning or maybe she was from the legal department, came up with the fact that, the first metre of land on the river bank, belonged to U.A.N.T. She could not understand how or where the ban on Rod's activities had come from.

When he pointed this, apparent, fact out to Mr Hutchins, he was astonished, and said that it was news to him. Another on-site meeting and Rod had put a notice in the boat window explaining about the ban on his activities. Most of the people who came past and read it were astonished at the harassment he was receiving. They waxed lyrical about how it brightened up the river and canal scene and thought that the boats, like his, should be encouraged. Not one of them saw any merit in the counter-argument of unfair competition.

Running the gauntlet of Bancroft basin was not as bad as usual because Mr. S. must have been on holiday. He had to go to the boat hire place to purchase the double license for the Avon. From what they said about his sales activities on the river it appeared that the major complainant had now become a committee member of U.A.N.T. That could explain the change in attitude. Wheels within wheels, infiltrate and corrupt, or should I say influence and, for the sake of avoiding being sued, corrupt as in to taint or alter.

A quick look around the premises of this boat hire place, revealed a small amount of dusty canal-ware. From the lack of display visible he imagined that their sales of canal-ware were virtually nil.

The attitudes of some people to somebody pursuing a different way of life seems almost unbelievable. The philosophy of live and let live was one which he had been brought up with as well as having been instilled with a strong sense of justice. His dislike of injustice had resulted, only about eighteen months before that, in him winning a twelve year long battle with Keighley police. An out of court settlement for damages of five thousand pounds plus costs had been won for assault and battery, after he had been wrongfully arrested whilst trying to report a crime to the police.* One of the reasons why he had chosen to live a simple life, on the canals was to get away from police harassment whilst he was pursuing the case and for a more peaceful life generally.

These, small-minded, troglodytes in Stratford, were irritations which he could do without. His strategy was to write to all the district council Chairpersons explaining his predicament. He sent them a brief summary of what his business was and an outline of the problems with regard to the river as well as photographs of the boat and his work. He subsequently received an acknowledgement from a council official, the same one who Mr. Hutchins had been dealing with, asking him to contact him about any proposed future visits.

The following year, before his visit, he phoned Mr. Hutchins who told him it that it was in the council's hands. Rod had to admit that his communication was a bit late because he was already on his way it up the river again. He phoned Mr. Wiggett, of the council, who told him that it was not possible to allow him to sell from the river bank. Pressing 'end' on his phone in despair he decided to phone the U.A.N.T. Chairman again. He said that he had been talking to Mr. Wiggett and was sorry to inform him that under no circumstances could they let him sell from the river bank again.

"This!" he said to Anne, "Could not be true! Was this the only response I was going to get from a council of fellow Liberals?"

All that Anne could say, with her usual, cynical appraisal of the human condition was

"It's money that's talking". Well!, if that was the case, there would be some more writing to do.

Whilst they travelled the last few miles up to Stratford he drafted another letter to the councillors which, it was intended, would be sent on his arrival. He phoned Mr. Wiggett again to inform him of his decision.
"No.!", he instructed, "Don't do that! If you are going to write again, then any correspondence has to go through me.!"
This now began to sound promising, so, he made it quite clear that his letters would go straight to the committee Chairperson's who he had written to before. It seemed as though it was only minutes after that phone call before Mr. Hutchins telephoned him again.
"I have just been having a word with Mr. Wiggett and he informed me that it has been decided to allow you to sell from the river bank on our usual terms!?"
After thanking him, he tried to question him about, the fastest U-turn in history. The only, slight explanation, which he could get from him was that he did not like to fall out with anybody, and that he had to live with the people in Stratford.

The evidence was there. Not of any financial inducements but of pressure being applied on Mr. Hutchins by certain other members of the U.A.N.T. committee. The most damningly stark evidence was that, at least one of council officials was being coerced by some means or other into trying to act contrary to the elected councillors wishes. Those were now two, unlooked for, battles which had been won but the main one was still raging. It has already been mentioned about paying the BW license by VISA. and of the license being subsequently issued. The year after that, in ninety seven, he sent a cheque with a photocopied renewal form to B.W. two months before the renewal date. The idea was that if they sent his cheque back he could lodge it with his solicitors with a view to either taking them to court for breach of contract or proof that the money had been tendered if they took him to court and also, possibly, for issuing a counter claim for breach of contract.

The cheque cleared, but about three months later, they sent him one of their cheques saying that they would not renew the license until he agreed to abide by their restrictions on where sales could take place. They received the cheque back, torn up, with yet another letter again stating that their requests were in breach of the agreement and that they were also illegal. No actual license was issued for Crete that year but BW took no action against him except for the usual harassment.

The next year, which was in nineteen ninety eight, he paid cash for his license at Goole Boathouse. The receipt which he was given was put in the window but again that year no license was issued. By this time B.W. had reviewed their license structure and had introduced a new trading license. The conditions of this new license included a list of places, all-over the country, where travelling boats could not sell from. It included everywhere that any reasonable sales could be made. They wrote to him again saying that the commercial licenses were strictly for carrying goods, and not for selling from the boat with. They said that he must change over to the trading license and abide by its restrictions. BW even suggested that they could find him a permanent mooring with good trade prospects if he would give up the commercial license battle.

They did not seem to understand that boats are made to move and that if he wanted to stay in one place he would probably be in the house. The person who was now writing to Rod had been given a specific mandate, to sort out his case. He wrote saying that there were three options. One was to take the new trading license with all its restrictions. The second was to take up their offer of a permanent mooring and enter into an agreement with that area's management. The third was to stop trading and buy a pleasure boat license.

He wrote back saying that those were not options and that the only options he would consider would be to carry on, as he was, under the existing agreement. The second option for them was to offer him sufficient compensation to make it worth his while to give up the contract. He tried to explain that their new trading license was barely suitable for someone, painting canal-ware as a hobby and that his turnover even when selling in the most popular places, for a couple of weeks year, was only about fifteen thousand pounds. Trying to explain to them that far from putting up all these obstacles in the way of travelling crafts boats they should be subsidizing them and encouraging them as canal attractions. It was like talking to someone from another planet.

"Ice creams, baguettes and the like, are high profit, a high turnover businesses". He told him. "Craft work of any kind is labour intensive and low turnover. You cannot treat them in the same way!"

British Waterways are aware of this when it comes to holding exhibitions. They charge for ice cream and food stalls, but in the prestige events, they will pay a painter to demonstrate their art..

"Can't you see?" he asked, "That in travelling crafts boats the Inland Waterways have the best, virtually free, ambassadors. People love to see us! They ask why they do not see more such attractions."

B.W. look on his boat and similar enterprises as a problem. Any good management will look laterally at a problem and turn it to their advantage. He was certain that he was not a problem, it was B.W. who were the problem. They have created the problem by having illegal contracts with waterside shops giving them sole rights to sell a traditional product on a particular stretch of canal. These were some of his main arguments. He went further than that and laid his cards on the table with regards the legal arguments which he would use in any court case. Namely the 1950s Wall's ice-cream case precedent and the fact that a contract exists until such time as his turnover exceeds seventeen thousand five hundred pounds on BW's waterways.

He was worried, and in truth, his solicitor, despite the fact that she advised him to continue with his business, had said that she was not sure how far BW's powers allowed them to go in the matter of waterway by-laws. Disputes had never really been put to the test as far as the High Court and House of Lords were concerned where precedent was the main thing. Cases would either be won or lost by default, with one or other of the parties backing down.

When he reached Stratford in ninety seven and Andrew Stumpf cautioned him about the unlicensed boat and threatened to confiscate it he began to see a court battle of no certain outcome, looming. Earlier that year when he had, again, stopped for a few days at Stoke Bruerne and the lock keeper asked him to move on but admitted that he was not going to take any action because Mr S. was going to resolve the matter if Rod dared to stop in Stratford again. He had similar intimations of doom from other Waterways officials who accosted him but took no action.

This was it then! The final showdown! Metaphorical pistols at ten paces. The weeks rolled on, the season ended, but there was as yet no summons in the post. Winter saw them in Goole again where Rod was working on 'Wylam', the shapely ex lead carrying coastal vessel renamed Maggie, which he and Anne had bought in Newcastle on Tyne in the autumn of ninety six.
After Stratford he did the usual circuit of the Bristol Channel the Kennet and Avon Canal and the Thames before heading off north, up the Grand Union Canal. It was when they were about to moor at Berkhamsted where he had last seen Dusty.
"Just take her in slowly," he asked Anne as he went forward to jump off with the front rope.

He jumped, but as he did so, his eye caught a glimpse of her boat, moored a few yards further ahead, on the other side of the canal.
"Keep going!" he instructed, frantically, as he jumped back on to the bows.

"How did you manage that?" Anne asked, in an air of total astonishment, when he returned to the stern.

"Manage what?" he asked. To which she replied,

"When you jumped off with the rope you turned back in mid-air and landed on the boat again without your feet touching the ground.

"Dusty always said that she was a witch" he answered, and he did not stop until they were on the summit.

chapter eighteen

all at sea with wylam

Before they met the barge Maggie, as she had been renamed from her original name of Wylam, they both imagined a blunt tubby craft which would look like a cross between a slurry boat and an oil platform because in the advert she had been described as a Goole barge. It was not the case because she was a very shapely ship with pointed bows and a sweeping round stern.

It was the price which attracted them. The owner desperately wanted to sell and had been gradually dropping his price so the temptation to consider purchasing this sixty foot by twenty foot, Goole Barge, as he called it, became attractive. The time was not the right one. When does the 'ideal' purchase come along when you want it?

They were living in a small caravan in the middle of a building site with prehistoric like, monsters, constantly feeding hungry juggernauts which roared around them as they arrived empty and went away satiated and sounding more angry at their departure than on their arrival.

This questionable residence was in order to enable them to carry out the commission of painting to a Dutch barge on the south London Docklands now known as Surrey Quays.
'Maggie' was in Newcastle on Tyne. Rod's car was in a garage in Bath having major shell replacement surgery.
"Let's get a coach and go and look at it". Enthused Anne.
"I have a better idea, my eldest daughter, Bronia, works in Sunderland, I'll, ask her to look at it for us". Was Rod's lacklustre response. With his, get out, in hand they continued with the painting when the weather was fine, wet and drying in the rain and cursing in the wind and the rain.

"It's quite good!" said Bronia, on the phone a few days later, and then modified her assessment as, "Well, it's got potential and lots of space" "You would probably like it. It has a six cylinder Gardener" he relayed to Anne,
"OH!" A garden!" she squealed almost bursting with the female impulse to purchase. A day return from London to the home of 'Newkie' Brown by National Express coach is almost a full twenty four hours. The photographs which Bronia and Peter had forwarded were very encouraging. It looked nothing like their worst visualization. It gave the impression of a seagoing ship or rather a car ferry with it's

several tiers of superstructure, but then again, when they eventually did see it with its tall masts and flying bridge it looked more like a child's drawing of an imaginary Tunisian car ferry.

Bill arranged to meet them at the bus station. The coach arrived in Newcastle early so Anne dashed off at a slow pace, doubled up with stomach cramps, to find a Veganin purveyor. Rod waited and waited and waited. Ten cigarettes later, in an effort to make up for the nicotine deprivation of the long trip, neither Anne nor Bill had appeared. He phoned Anne but her battery must have been dead and he could get no answer.

At her eventual return, and with no sign of Bill, they wandered away from the coach station to try and find where this wonderful Maggie was moored. After fruitless searching of the immediate waterfront on the part of the river which they found they hailed a taxi which cost them nearly as much as the return coach trip. Anne's cramps had gone but his Victor Meldrew impersonation began to surpass anything on television.

There it was in all its, unquestionably, grotesque splendour. The interior was 1950s kitsch, "Mandela House!" Anne whispered to him as the proud builder of this superstructure showed them round. A generator clattered endlessly from the stern and piped, radio 2 music invaded every quarter. It was mid-afternoon in September and although it was a bright afternoon every light inside and outside this vessel was blazing forth. From the top to the bottom the craft could be described briefly, thus:- the bridge, a vast expanse of steel surrounded by thin steel shuttering and hand rails with a wheel in the front, just a wheel, not connected to the rudder, no throttle or gear change connections. This looked out onto the roof of the rest of the accommodation. Over the stern was a sheer drop of some twenty five feet on to the mud of this tidal mooring on a derelict industrial wharf. There was only one other boat, apparently its sister ship, which had been ballasted well down into the water and was being fitted out as a yacht by an octogenarians for him to sail round the world.

The mud flats, of the ebbed tide, were splendid in their isolation and variety of bird life. On the far shore were new office developments which would, no doubt, soon invade this site now almost reclaimed by nature. Below the flying bridge was the main accommodation.
"I like the layout,!" Commented Anne.
"It's well insulated", Bill informed them with pride.

It was a very liveable space. The bathroom had a duck egg blue suite, there was a kitchen with all the fittings and an adjacent breakfast room. A double bedroom with a large wardrobe and a car radio from whence all the scattered speakers were emanating. The lounge was the 'coup de gras'. A new nineteen fifties gas fire faced them from the far side of the cabin where the ceiling height came down to about five foot. On the right was a bar with its optics and mock beer dispensers. To the left of the door stood a one armed bandit. Two large ceramic pigs sat on either side of the fire, and, even they, had a startled expression on their faces as they surveyed the ornate mirrors advertising everything from stout to real estate. Above the pigs were Renaissance ceramic figures who refused to acknowledge anything before them but preferred to remain in isolated splendour. All this was built above the gunnel's level of this, deep hulled, ex lead carrying coastal vessel.

The hold was a maze of cabins, workshops and a large engine room with a carpet on the floor round the engine which did not match the bright colours in which the machinery had been painted. Surrounding this surreal sight was a turmoil of wires, batteries, connectors and battery charges with the detritus of engineering and electrical junk. Through a large door, which was cut into what used to be the stern ballast tank, a large Lister generator rattled on incessantly. A series of holes had been cut out of the hull above the water line to ventilate the source of power. Bill instructed him in the art of power sharing.
"To change the batteries you plug that one into that one there; but; if you want to charge those, which are your twelve volt, which are actually fifteen volt, so that they can use the twenty four volt charger, because I have not got a twelve volt charger, you put that into that, and then, when the power is needed for the twenty four volt lights", etc., etc,.etc.,.

"What do you do to start engine". Rod inquired. Bill confidently changed yet more of the heavy-duty industrial bayonet plugs and pressed the engine starter button. Whirr, Whirr went the solenoid but failed to turn the engine. Without a moment's hesitation he changed the connection from the twelve volt to the twenty four, come fifteen volt, and hesitantly the engine started. That lovely piece of engineering ran much more sweetly than the colours it was painted. By this time the tide had come in sufficiently to engage gear which Bill did by pushing forward the three foot long gear leaver with the bright red knob.

The splendour of its performance and its thrust against the straining ropes and chains which secured it to the bank, momentarily blinded Rod from all the defects of conception and construction which Bill was so proud off. The wiring which hung like Christmas trimmings throughout the hold; the plugs, every one of which was 15 amp, with a different label bearing, 12 volt, 24 volt and 240 volt stickers. The 240 volt lights which came on with the generator and had no switches to turn them off. The gas system which had three separate bottles connected with a mixture of rubber, plastic and copper piping, going to various water and room heaters around the boat was totally unsafe and the pipes were draped like festive bunting as they vanished into the ceiling and then out again after supplying one fitting or another in the upper deck. The water system had three tanks on the bridge which gravity fed to the taps and water heaters. There were also two, in line, 12 volt pumps to boost the pressure for the Paloma water heaters. This was not strictly true. One of the pumps pushed the water from two of the tanks to one of them. The other one then stepped up the pressure to the water heater in the kitchen or pushed it across, through the kitchen water heater and then through the bathroom water heater, to get really hot water for the bath. 'Fred Carno'! Look to your laurels, Bill is about. A four hundred gallon water container, in the hold, had a 240 volt pump to top up the aforementioned system. The ingenuity of Bill, the boat builder, was endless.

At about 5.30 pm.,. Bronia collected them so Rod asked Bill what his bottom price was.
"Scrap price!" he replied, in desperation..

They did not commit themselves and as they drove away in the gathering dusk, Maggie, rode the calm waters of the upper Tyne, for all the world like a well illuminated car ferry .
"I like the layout!" reaffirmed Anne. Rod's head was in his hands as they reversed away from Maggie's glaring lights and forty foot high masts with the security lights giving, yet another, dimension to its top-heavy appearance.

Back at Bronia and Peter's house after food and a few glasses of wine, Rod phoned Bill and said that they would take her on at the scrap price of £7.500.

Two weeks later after finishing the barge painting in London they took possession and began to uncover the full horrors of the boat which Bill built. The windows, wooden domestic ones, which he had installed a few inches above the water line had to be covered with steel plates, the engine controls were put up to the bridge and the engine cooling, which Bill had temporarily put through a calorifier, was again sea water cooling.

Anne was adamant about not helping to crew down the North Sea. Other friends and relations cried off or postponed due to various reasons. The main unspoken excuse, if the truth was known, was probably the same as Anne's spoken one.
"Go down the North sea in that hulk at this time off the year!". "You must be joking."
"This is a partnership", Rod had pleaded,
"Go bungee jumping if you want an adrenaline rush but don't involve me,". She concluded.

"Mutiny!" Rod shouted and Crew, their big brave dog, who does not like raised voices, left the ship and slunk off to the other end of the Wharf.

It took two weeks of frantic pottering round, at a snail's pace, before the ship was barely ready to make the journey. The list was endless, new batteries, repair the alternator, strap the gas bottles, cut up the masts, find ten tons of ballast, weld the cockpit seat into place, buy compass and charts, repair a diesel leak in the generator and finally Bill provided a ship to shore radio.

Terry and John arrived on a Saturday and Anne departed. They set off at high water at 1-30am. on that Sunday morning. The first obstacle which they had to overcome, or rather get under, was the Swing Bridge in Newcastle; it was only about two miles downriver from the moorings. It was a cold and frosty night with a clear sky but no moon. After casting off they practised manoeuvring her before setting off down the river. This was his first time out in Maggie. A week earlier, when Colette had been visiting, he had meant to have a trial run until Bill informed him that it was not possible to get off the mud bank on neap tides. Colette was disappointed but he had been quite relieved. The ropes were as thick as her arms and he didn't think that her and Anne, who was also visiting him, could have handled them.

Bel had brought Colette up to Newcastle to join Rod for a few days and had left her in his charge. He was pleased to try to involve and interest her in the work he was doing to prepare Maggie for the passage down the North Sea. Of particular fascination was a nut and bolt warehouse with large display boards around the walls occupied by groups of different sizes and shapes of all types of hardware fastenings as well as nuts and bolts.

"I wanted to go to the Metro Centre". Colette said bursting into tears as Rod was extolling the virtues of the displays.

"Oh!" said Rod somewhat taken aback at her outburst, "We will do that tomorrow then".

"Mum says that, if its ok with you, I can have my nose pierced", she assured him as they headed up the road to the Metro Centre the following day. 'Anything to keep her happy' Rod thought as he sat there waiting. It turned out that he had been conned because Bel had said No!. Bronia picked her up the following day to take the very happy child with the sleepers in her ears and nose home. Anne caught a train back to London.

So...with the controls set up on the flying bridge and all the systems apparently working they set off. She appeared to handle well. Well she handled a bit on the sluggish side with Bills improvised a hydraulic steering. They stopped at the sidings before the bridge and waited until half tide before, successfully, going under the bridge. Apart from the weather being very cold and ice forming on everything, the journey to the fisheries at North Shields was, until they were manoeuvring to tie up, uneventful. The fishing boats were leaving the jetty so he slowed down for them to get out of the way. A wake caught them, broadside on, and the boat lurched alarmingly.

"God!" he thought. 'If this is what she is going to do with just the wash from another boat, what the hell is she going to do at sea..

"It is because we are not moving," reassured Terry, probably as much for his own peace of mind. John said nothing.

They tied up carefully in the icy conditions. Whilst John and Rod moved as many heavy articles as they could find on the upper deck into the hold, Terry inflated his dingy and put his dry suit on.

"This is not a very reassuring", commented John as Terry checked his air bottles and almost put his flippers on.

"If anything does happen." Terry observed, "I will be the one to rescue you before you died of hypothermia".

"Anyone fancy a beer?" Rod offered but neither of them did, and, nor did he'..

They cast off, but John, who had been untying a rope on the wharf, was left behind. They did full circle and picked him up but the starboard navigation light, which Bill had fixed on the flying bridge's full width, was claimed as a trophy by the wharf.

"Another Bill job!" the three of them said in unison. The radio, which appeared to work when Bill had demonstrated it, also refused to contact anybody.

As they left Tynemouth on a perfectly calm sea and a clear blue sky in the, still early morning, the fog swallowed them up.

"Sound the horn every minute," Rod instructed John. A good morning fart would have been more audible than the lesser squeak emanating from yet another Bill job.

"Why don't you keep a straight course?" Terry kept saying, as Rod struggled with the sluggish steering in a calm sea of fog.

"For God sake man, you're twenty degrees to port now". Terry was getting rattled, and John brought up more coffees from the galley, sorry, Dell Boys, kitchen.

"John...", instructed Terry, "...go to the stern and shout up when the rudder is dead centre so that we can mark it on the wheel".
They carried out this exercise, whilst he corrected the wheel, until Terry was satisfied. "It's your turn at the wheel now Terry!" said Rod, "See if you can do any better".

They were, more or less, on course as Rod handed over. Terry held the, raffia covered peeling chrome wheel, in his allotted centre position and they did a full, quite tight circle to port. His language was blue as he corrected it again and then held her steadily on a slightly wider circle to starboard.
"It's another Bill job," said John as a coaster came out of the fog and narrowly missed them, John took a turn at steering so Rod went below to find Terry making sandwiches and taking his pills. He made his way back on deck and after, unsuccessfully trying not to piss into the wind, found John was going round in continuous circles.
"Are you all right?", he asked him as he was bent over the compass.
"This compass is not right, " John observed, " It is going round in circles".

The fog was disorientating but as Rod pointed out to him, that if he looked at the wake, which could just be seen, it was ellipsing. As Terry emerged with the sandwiches and coffee he mused about them being observed on radar.
"The 'Navy Lark' lives again," "They will be absolutely pissing themselves." he said. Several hours later they thought that they caught a glimpse of Sunderland, which was several hours later than it should have been. The engine ran as sweet as a, nut, and the engine room was

also the warmest place on the boat so that every time that he went to check on it Rod stayed longer than was necessary.

By early afternoon the fog had still not lifted. Terry was doing the chart reading and he was concerned that they might be too far east and suggested that they take a more southerly course. Rod did not agree but he was outvoted by the two of them. It was his turn to steer again whilst they went to warm up. They had been gone about half an hour when he sensed a change in the sound of the sea. It was an unnerving sound of quietness,. he eased the throttle back just as the fog cleared momentarily to reveal cliff's and a beach, with occasional rocky islets, sticking menacingly out of the water no more than a hundred yards away.

It was full throttle and hard to port and then took as steady a course as he had taken that day, due East! Some three-quarters of an hour later Terry and John emerged with food and coffee. Rod was still heading due East.
"You are on the wrong course!" observed Terry.
"You bet I am" was Rods terse reply, still shaking, as he related the previous hours observations.
"Oh! Good!", replied their navigator, "We were not too far out then!"
 The fog cleared a bit in the early afternoon and the horn, which must have been suffering from frostbite, thawed out and started working. The, 'Bill special' radio never did repeat its brief performance but they had mobile phones with the relevant emergency numbers on memory. Hartlepool was a welcoming sight and because the weather was forecast to blow up they decided to stay until the predicted storms had blown over.

Whilst Terry and Rod, after the usual hassle of retrieving a car from the departure point, drove off to rescue Terry's narrow boat which was broken down on the river Soar, John volunteered to look after Maggie and carry out a few maintenance jobs. Over the following five days, the storms raged, and the mooring fees mounted, so that, when the wind dropped and the forecast was favourable they chugged out of Hartlepool Marina. This was very much to the relief of several marina residents whose power had been persistently cut off several times whilst they were welding the steel window shutters on more securely.

Terry, whose self-preservation instinct had kicked into top gear, had purchased a hand held G.P.S and short-wave ship to shore radio. It was just before midnight when they locked out on a rising tide to avoid having to pay yet another days mooring fees. There was barely a breeze and although they knew that the seas would probably still be fairly high after the previous days gales they were horrified by the size of the swell when Maggie left the sheltered waters of the bay.

The swell caught them broadside on to their course so for a while they changed direction to head north-east into the mountainous seas. Their position on the flying bridge was some twenty feet above the water or least it had been when the water stayed still. When they were in the hollow of the waves they could not see over the tops of the waves on either side of them whilst the exaggerated whiplash effect of their height above the centre of gravity forced them to hold onto the wheel or crawl about holding on to anything they could.

During the first few rolls and pitching it seemed as though she might capsize but after a short while it became evident that the ballast calculations were correct. John came staggering then crawling onto the bridge with two mugs of tea. By the time he reached them the mugs were empty. The sound of the seas drowned their laughter as efficiently as its turbulence had taken away the tea. Then, to confound the situation, there seemed to be no response from the rudder and soon they were being turned and battered, powerless, broadside on to the relentless sea.
"We've lost the effing steering!", Rod shouted, soundlessly, to his companions. It was only minutes, but ones which seemed like hours, before Terry discovered that John, whilst crawling along the deck he had been holding on to the manual gear connecting rod and had accidentally put the boat into neutral.

By the time we were under way again their heading was back to Hartlepool. They took a diagonal course, riding the waves, which was almost pleasurable by comparison with the previous hour. They debated whether to return to calmer waters but eventually decided that,
"If she can take the pounding which we have already experienced we might as well resume our planned course". The swell seemed to be relentless, but, as the night progressed there was a noticeable diminution in the height of the waves. When they had made the decision to continue John bravely volunteered to crawl away and make another pot of tea. Crew, whilst all these seas had been rolling and rocking them, had been curled up on a life ring on the bridge deck. She had bagged her buoyancy and was sticking to it.

The galley, which was at the stern of the accommodation deck, had its doors opening on to the rear deck. The ladder up to the flying bridge was reached across the heaving deck and came out on the flying bridge at the farthest most point away from the wheel. Johns second attempt at delivering pots of tea to them was three-quarters successful. Rod and Terry took one sip and immediately, as though it had been rehearsed, threw the contents of the mugs, one to port and the other to starboard, with such violence that John, who was not feeling too happy with his current world, thought that his friends had turned against him as well. John, who liked three sugars in his tea, had assumed that because of the stressful conditions they might be in need of added energy.
"Hell!" they said as they flung in unison. "Are you trying to bloody well poison us?" Rod left Terry at the wheel, and left John, holding on to the hand rail and his hurt feelings, to make a fresh pot of drinkable tea.

The pounding waves broke one of the window covers free. This heavy plate of 5 ml. steel, somehow became tangled up in a fender rope, so, instead of it falling into the ocean it was swinging violently and crashing into the side of the boat. Before the sea had a chance to break the flimsy window glass, this, self evolved, battering ram smashed it with great efficiency. John and Rod cut it free whilst Terry took the wheel. The generator was started up to give them light in the hold, which was taking quite a lot of water through the large broken window. John went in one direction, looking for nails, whilst Rod found a suitable piece of three-quarter inch plywood and wedged it up with a plank. Fore and aft he searched for John, then, on to the main deck before clambering up to the flying bridge. He could not be found.

"I haven't seen him." Terry said,

"I've looked everywhere".

"GOD! He must have gone overboard!". Said Rod with an increasing tone of panic. Terry pressed the key to save the position on the G P.S whilst Rod dashed off crab wise across the deck to go below and have yet another look for John.

'Ann will kill me if I've lost him' Rod mused, but, there he was holding the large board up against the broken window wondering where Rod had got to.

"That was an early bath!", John wryly observed after they had secured the board and doubly firmed it into place with wedged ladders.

"That should get us a Blue Peter badge" they agreed as the bilge pump, rapidly cleared the sea, back to where it belonged.

As dawn broke Rod volunteered to take the first sleep and left them on watch. It was difficult to stay on the bed, but after discovering that a total spread out position, prevented him from rolling off it, he slept fitfully alternating from being, now stood on his feet and then his head. He was woken up once by an excessive lurch and momentarily saw a ship speeding past in the opposite direction. he went to sleep again, but, when he did wake up and realize that it was the starboard side that this other ship had passed them on, he thought that he had better go up to the bridge and investigate. After rolling out of the bed he dashed up to the bridge just in time to see another ship heading straight for them.

Terry, who had his 'RYA. Yacht master Ocean', certificate, was heading over to port, chuntering.

"Every time I go over, he shadows my action"

"FOR CHRIST SAKE!". Rod shouted, grabbing the wheel from him at the same time and going had to starboard.

"Port to Port!".

Of all the events of that voyage it is that one which makes him wake up in a cold sweat. Terry must have been very tired and probably a little seasick. He had taken his seasick pills after they had set off when he should have taken them an hour or two before. Other than that he was trying to commit suicide and take them with him.

The ships passed each other, port to port, with inches to spare. They were eyeball to eyeball with a crew member on the deck. The captain in that much larger vessel was not going to give way to Terry's game of chicken, as the other one, which he had seen from his bed must have done. He would have sunk them, and, he would have been in the right. Terry turned in for a much-needed sleep after that whilst John and Rod continued in silent concentration.

The G.P.S. turns plotting a course into child's play, so, with this, the calmer seas and a ship to follow on the horizon, which was obviously on the same course as them, he left John at the wheel. After doing the rounds in the engine room and staying down there, for short-time warming up, he returned to find John going round in circles again.

"Its Bills steering!", he said when the fact was pointed out to him.

"Yes!", Rod agreed, "but it's like steering an old banger" Rod started to explain but, before he could finish the simile he was interrupted with.

"You should know about 'Old bangers'!"
"I'll tell Anne you said that!" Rod retorted.
"I'll tell Anne about your old bangers, if you do!" Was this 'humorously' blackmailing reply.

By mid- afternoon, and with the sea a comparatively gentle swell, they were well on their way to Spurn Head. John gave up his attempts at steering but, with the drinking water running low, he pumped up water from the large tank in the hold. Shortly after that he supplied them with more coffees on the bridge.
"That's not drinkable". Terry and Rod observed, yet again, in unison.
"You are always complaining! What's wrong with it now?". John asked in desperation, feeling that his efforts were very much undervalued.
"Its got a chemical taste!", said Terry.
"It tastes like old engine oil!", Rod analysed and John had to agree, when he tasted it, that they were right. After relaying where the water had come from they all agreed.
"It's another Bill job!". The old pump which Bill had fitted was leaking oil in to the water as it pumped it.

Dusk had fallen as they rounded Spurn head and radioed the Humber pilot to find out about any shipping hazards.
"You can take any course you want!", was the reassuring reply to Terry who then plotted the course to Hull.
Rod went below to do the usual engine room checks and try to flush out the fuel filters. They were running on the slow side, but he did not like to stop the engines to change it filters because the batteries did not seem to be charging very well. On his return to the bridge, the lights, for the main channel were about a mile to Port and the near

blackness of a land mass loomed ahead in the darkness of the fast fallen autumn day.

"Are you sure we are on the right course?". Rod questioned Terry.
"Of course we are,! Look there is a channel marker flashing ahead"
"That's not a channel marker it's a dust cart with a flashing orange light" Rod observed wryly as a solitary car headlight could be seen about half a mile ahead travelling horizontally to their course.
"That's definitely land ahead" Rod insisted as Terry went off down below grumbling that his G P.S could not be wrong. He took over and headed, to port, across the mud flats which he visualized from the previously studied chart, and took them back to where the Channel lights could be seen. To this day, Terry will not admit, that he had plotted the course directly from Spurn to Hull, overland..

They reached Hull just after high tide and took refuge in the marina until the following incoming tide at the request of the lock keeper who told them that it would not be safe to tie up outside on the river. Crew, who had refused to use an improvised litter tray of soil on the back deck, leapt off the vessel and squatted in a self-made sauna. She wee'd and wee'd, with the steam from her retentive bladder gradually enveloping her on that frosty night.

"To the pub!". Rod said with half-hearted enthusiasm.
"No!", they replied with greater enthusiasm, not to do so. After they had eaten and brewed a cup of tea with oil-less water, what little non-enthusiasm they had to go out for a drink, turned into instant sleep.

They were woken at about 5 am., with only a few minutes to go before they had arranged to lock out, so, there was no time to change the oil filters.

At Ocean lock in Goole they, quite fortunately, whilst waiting to go in, had breasted up with Brian Hunts working barge, because the fuel starved Gardener could hardly stem the tide into the loch. So! There the three of them were, in Goole, bonded through self-imposed hardship. All that Rod had to do now was to get his narrowboat to Goole where he could live whilst refitting Maggie.

Rod had not heard anything from the, ever threatening, Mr. Stumpf and the time was fast approaching when the license, which he had not seen for two years, was due to be renewed. British Waterways are, probably, quite skilled at chasing money which is owed to them but seemed unable to cope with someone paying them unwanted license renewals. 'They were, probably' he thought, 'on the lookout for him trying to pay by one of the methods that he had paid in the previous year's.' This was proved correct when Paul, the marina owner at Goole, told him that he had received instructions not to take any more renewals for commercial licenses. With this in mind he set up a standing order using the bank details which he had kept, on record, from the cheque which they had tried to repay the tendered renewal money with a couple of years before.

Towards the end of February, very much to their surprise, they received a renewal notice for the Commercial license, the first in three years, in the post from Watford. This was duly filled in and returned with a note explaining the method which had been used to pay them. It took three

months of letters and phone calls before their super efficient system could trace the standing order payment. A license was eventually received in the post.
At about the same time they received a communication from British Waterways solicitors at Towcester informing him that they had applied to the court to have the matter, which had been adjourned sine die, removed from the register.

On their summer visit to Stratford, that year, they were welcomed by U.A.N.T. but, suffered an ominous silence when in Bancroft basin. The lock keeper would walk past them in the morning and, quite purposefully, look away. Towards the end of the second week Rod could not stand this rebuttal any longer
"Good morning!".he accosted him so that the lock keeper had to acknowledge him.
"Huh!" he grunted, "I haven't seen you.!" he contradicted himself as he continued about his business.
Everybody, one of Rods philosophies goes, should change their career or at least every ten years, so that now B.W. has taken away the driving interest, the adrenaline rush, of painting and selling canal-ware, across the towpath, He decided to move on to bungee jumping or sky diving. 'It can never be quite as exciting as the B.W. battle, but, I can't have everything', he thought.

chapter nineteen

all at sea... again!

It was two years before he went out on the canals again in Crete. It had been a busy two years during which time, with the help of several people, he had completely rebuilt and refitted the cabin structure on the now renamed Wylam. The crowning glory of this was a wonderful new, shiny mahogany wheel house. This had all been achieved in between being unable to work because of a bad back, a bad knee and a stiff neck and purchasing, decorating and furnishing five cheap houses between them in Goole, which he and Anne had calculated should give a reasonable return on their investment.

(Anne says he should put up more sex and shopping into the story, so, there we are, they bought five houses and refurbished them. Just too knackered for the sex after all that).

Before I go on to describe his brief return to selling the canal-ware from Crete, in what he now thought was an established accepted business, I must describe briefly the not uneventful trip which saw him take Wylam from Goole to London Docklands.

They set off at the end of July 99. The weather forecast was a little indifferent with winds of three to four, increasing to five later, was in force when they commenced their journey. The motley crew consisted of himself, Anne as reluctant passenger, Crew the dog, Charlie the cat, Frank as skipper, Chris 'the vicar of Dibley', Who was a stowaway and Franks mistress, Paul as engineer with Ted and John as cabin boys. All seemed to be going well, until, on one occasion, as he returned to the wheel house from the engine room he heard on a the ship's radio the Humber coast guard signing off after broadcasting a message to all shipping.

"What was that Frank?" Rod asked.
"Just an update on the weather " Franks said.
"What did they say?". Rod asked.
"I think it was about the same as before ". Frank replied.
"Can we get back to them and check the details " Rod asked.
"No! We don't want to bother them " said Frank terminating the conversation.

Some two hours later the 'force seven' which had been forecast as imminent, hit them.

'Not again,' Rod thought, as Wylam lurched, rolled and juddered in the freshly whipped up angry sea. The boat could obviously take the pounding, but, some of the items which had been tied down broke loose. The microwave in the wheel house galley was one of these items, and, at about the same time Chris lost her footing. The microwave and Chris were chasing each other backwards and forwards across the wheel house floor. Nobody could catch either of them for some time. Crew kept losing her footing and sliding backwards down the steps into the lower deck. Annie eventually wedged herself at the top of the steps and held on to Crew. A couple of hours into this raging storm the steering packed in completely. They were adrift in very heavy seas without steering. The emergency steering buckled under the pressure and an attempt to steer the vessel. A large still-son wrench and a length of scaffolding failed to make much impression on their inability to steer a course as two of them, on their backs, were being pushed across the deck as they tried to steer a course.

"Don't you think we ought to send out a Mayday? ". Rod asked Frank.

"I suppose we could do" agreed Frank who seemed reluctant to use the radio.

A large gas bottle which had been tied on to the hand rails on the back deck broke loose and was trying to kill anybody who ventured out on to the deck before they managed to propel it overboard. After another two hours of being tossed around in mountainous seas which were even worse than the ones were when leaving Hartlepool they were eventually taken under tow by the powerful Humber lifeboat. Two one inch thick steel hawsers were

roped to them across the raging seas as they struggled to keep a foothold on the bows as they were secured through the two openings at either side of the bows to create cross straps to help to keep Wylam on a straight course. After only a short time one of them snapped.
"Go forward and retie the remaining one in a straight line" instructed the lifeboat skipper over the radio.
Paul and Ted volunteered to do that task and they watched, horrified as Ted was nearly washed over board before being pulled back by Paul.
"What happens if that one snaps" Rod enquired over the radio.
"You will have to abandon ship" came back the reply.

Wylam swung in a wide arc from side to side as she was towed, unsteerable, back to Grimsby at a greater speed than she could manage under her own steam. Much to the astonishment of the terrified crew, Rod spread eagled himself on the couch and went to sleep saying that there was nothing to do now that they were under tow

The following morning after they had gained entrance to Grimsby harbour the crew, except for John, left hurriedly like rats leaving a sinking ship. The two of them took three days to rebuild the steering anchorage. In order to continue the journey they found two, out of work fishermen, who volunteered to crew on the voyage and George from Goole, the engineer who had designed the faulty steering.

The two fishermen were a double act straight out of a comedy. It turned out that one of them was a cook and the other a ships hand. Their humour was a kind of homophobic banter which they obviously used to cover up the fact that they were gay partners. The act although obvious to Rod was probably to cover up the fact when at sea with a manly crew they would not be suspected of being what they were. 'Everybody must have seen through it' Rod thought.

Anne was pleased to re-join him in London but swore that she would never go to sea again in Wylam. They spent the rest of that year and the following spring finishing and fitting out of the lower decks.

chapter twenty

boat hooks at dawn

'It was time', Rod thought, 'to take Crete out onto the canals again for a couple of months to sell some of the stock which had remained unsold from the canal-ware venture. 'The show is not over until the fat lady sings'. Who the fat lady is, he had not yet found out but one bright summer morning in 'that year of our Lord two thousand', a rounded patrol officer had him towed away from the centre of Birmingham for the second time in a week. It was an acute attack of déjà vu but with a difference. It was the last straw.

Without hesitation he went straight down to the County court and took out an action in the form of a small claim for ' breach of the implied terms of the contract'. The contract being the 1992 agreement and the implied terms were that he should be able to make a living selling canal-ware from his boat under that agreement. BW's breach was that by denying him reasonable access to busy locations they made it impossible for him to make living. The damages which he sought were for loss of earnings of a thousand pounds by being unlawfully towed away from that busy location and for harassment over the eight years of the agreement. One of the main planks of his case was that BW's actions were anti-competitive and against the public interest both for denying him reasonable access to busy locations and for denying those with Low Intensity Trading licenses similar access.

Documents were exchanged and the date for the hearing was fixed for April 24th. 2001. His searches through the" All England Law reports " for precedents proved fruitless and even a record of a case which he remembered from the 1950s where, Wall's ice-cream tried to stop the ice-cream vans selling within a mile of their retail outlets, could not be found. BW, he had heard, nearly always settled out of court to avoid precedent. Maybe, he mused, they would offer to buy him out, as he had suggested to them a few years before, rather than let this matter go to court.

In his research he came across cases which mentioned the OFT's anti competitive practices investigation department, so, he sent a file to them asking them to investigate British Waterways Board. The results were not very encouraging because the Department just seemed to accept everything which BW said to them, almost without question, and just wrote back to him reiterating the Board's line. His replies to the OFT pointed out where BW were misleading them but it seemed that in the final analysis an investigation did not fall within the anti competitive branches remit because BW did not control more than 40% of the market.

When the case which he had brought against BW came to court in April the exchange of letters between himself and the OFT was still continuing but with very little hope of any positive result. Tuesday April 24th.01 crept up slowly and then seemed to leap upon him very quickly. When he was called into the courtroom it was quite small and very informal in the Small Claims hearing. There were no oaths, no statements of affirmation but just a down-to-earth presentation of the facts and claims. He and Anne had driven to Birmingham County Court from London and despite allowing three hours for what he thought should be an hour and a half journey they arrived, breathless, with minutes to spare.

There were five or six reporters there who had responded to his press release about the case. The first thing which Miss Greta O'Shea the BW legal executive did was to submit to the judge that the Press should not be allowed into the court because the case was a private matter, and that the press might give BW bad publicity. After a short hearing, in chambers, the judge, without any hesitation ruled that the hearing was in open court and that BW had no valid reason to object to the press being there.

The witnesses for the BW were Gordon Preece and Albert Rooke. Rod had Anne who, after he had presented the case as previously outlined, gave witness to Andrew Stumpf turning potential customers away whilst they had been moored in Stratford those few years earlier. None of the other boaters, who had a similar agreement with BW to Rods, turned up to be witnesses as they had promised.

Miss O'Shea, for BW, denied that a contract existed from 92 and claimed that the correspondence leading up to the issuing of the commercial license was not relevant and that the license was only issued annually to carry goods and did not give permission to sell goods across the towpath. Gordon Preece gave great emphasis on the mooring sign saying ' Maximum Stay' 48 hours and said that the £5 per day charge for overstaying was not an invitation to stay any longer than the maximum of 48 hours.

1pm. was fast approaching, so whilst Miss O'Shea was presenting her case Rod, quietly, asked Anne if she would go and feed the parking meter and take crew out for a walk. When all the preliminary evidence had been presented the judge adjourned the hearing for luncheon, Rod had to pose for press photos outside the court before dashing off to find Anne and the car. He got to the car but Crew was still locked in and there was no sign of Anne who had the car key. He telephoned her mobile to mobile and learned that she was lost and still, over half an hour later, looking for the car. How is it? he asked himself. That woman have no sense of direction. They eventually met up with the only just enough time for him to get back to court without even having had time for a coffee, leaving Anne pointing in the correct direction to find the car and take Crew for a walk.

After lunch the defence gave a her final presentation. She had not really got it together and struggle to find her references. Occasionally, in between reading some relevant sections of BW regulations and veering off into irrelevant passages, she quoted passages from correspondence which clearly supported Rods case. She did terminate these slips while searching for passages which supported her case. She seemed to go on interminably while sometimes apologizing and asking for a little more time, and, even an adjournment to put BW's case together. The judge refused this and insisted that he would like to finish the case and give judgement at that hearing.

Anne returned sometime during the two hours of Greta O'Shea's presentation. She had found the car and taken Crew for a walk, but was drenched the skin with the persistent heavy rain. At about the same time as Anne returned Rod noticed that the pen which he was taking notes with was leaking. he had, as one does, brushed his hair back with his hand or maybe scratched his nose or leaned momentarily, head in hand, with the result that the ink had been transferred to various parts of his face. This, almost certainly ruined the image which the unaccustomed suit and borrowed tie had created.

It must have been about 4pm by the time Miss O'Shea had finished and Rod's time came to sum up for himself as plaintiff. Despite making copious notes of points to raise, he felt that the judge's patience had worn thin with BWs protracted struggle to collate her case, so he was determined to try and pick up only on the really relevant points. By doing this he failed to emphasize the point of law that it is not a statutory offence to overstay the time limit on visitor moorings, but relied on evidence which was acknowledged by the defence that he had paid the overstay fee.

Needless to say, he put across as forcefully as he could, the fact that all the elements of contract were present in the agreement of 92. "offer acceptance and consideration", and submitted that, regardless of any changes in BW's license conditions that these could not change their agreement retrospectively. He accepted that BW's license was issued annually but submitted that these were the equivalent to a Road tax disc and separate to the agreement. He concluded his summing up as quickly as was possible and then there was an adjournment whilst the judge made his deliberations and Rod went off to the toilet to cleaned the ink off his face.

The judgement in cases always seems to start off by emphasizing points in favour of one side. It then, as a general rule, demolishes these claims and ends up, in a way, complementing the original assertions in such a way that they become negative rather than positive. It was just so in this judgement, to the extent that the early apparent support for the Board's case gave him great hope that the format would be followed. The judge decided that BW had full knowledge of the agreement which was the basis of the issuing of the commercial license and ruled that the exchange of letters did not constitute a contract but did give him the Board's permission to sell his canal-ware across the towpath under a commercial license as long as it continued to be reissued.
To that extent it appeared that the judge accepted that the board was in breach of that consent by trying to prevent him from selling goods across the tow path.

No judgement was given on BW's anti-competitive practices. This seemed to be, in part, because Miss O'Shea had tried to introduce a letter which BW had sent to the Office of fair Trading in reply to the OFT's inquiries which were instigated by his reports to them. Rod had objected to the production of that letter because of not having time to read it and because the matter was still, he hoped, being investigated by the Office of Fair Trading. The judge appeared to have ruled, at that time, that he would accept Rod's objections and would not include consideration of anti-competitive practices in his judgement if it was still being investigated by the OFT. He then went on to deliberate about BW towing his boat away. He decided that BW had a lawful right to tow 'Crete' away on the grounds that he accepted BW's definition of it being an obstruction to the visitor moorings. The Boards powers regarding the removal of boat's which they consider to be an obstruction say that they must give 28 days' notice to the owner before they can charge for the removal. BW's claim for costs was rejected.

Because the judge ruled that BW had removed his boat lawfully from Bindley Place he did not awarded him damages for loss of earnings as a result of the removal. The judge did award him £200 in damages for loss of earnings because of harassment to himself and potential customers by Andrew Stumpf whilst in Stratford in 96. Rod was also awarded costs. It was a victory of sorts. At least a partial victory which left several questions still to be answered. Miss O'Shea asked the judge for leave to appeal but this was refused. The judge pointed out to Rod that he could ask him for his permission to appeal but he said that he was reasonably happy with the court's decision.

The fat lady has not yet sung.

The following spring the Commercial licence was issued but was followed shortly by a letter saying that it had been issued by mistake and could he return it and they would send him a refund.

"You must be joking!" he wrote back to them and refused to comply.

Never the less he had decided to terminate the canal painting and travelling round the system, so, 6 months later when he had sold Crete he contacted the licensing officer and was told that the full refund was still available if he returned it, which he did. The battle had, in a sense, been won and he must have been the only person to have had half a year free on the canals with the permission of BW. He has heard, over the subsequent years, that if ever his name came up at BW executive meetings that groans of despair emanated from certain quarters.

The plan to use Wylam as a hotel boat taking holiday makers between Windsor and London fell at the first hurdle because the information that the locks up to Windsor could accommodate a vessel of up to 6mtr beam which was given to him through the Office at Reading was incorrect. The lock above Sunbury was less than 6mtr.

As luck would have it they did not need to travel anywhere. As soon as they arrived in Poplar Dock marina they were bombarded with family and friends wanting to stay in their cabins and really happy to pay a decent contribution to the mooring fees and upkeep of the boat.

It all started whilst they were still in Goole getting ready to sail to London.

"What are you doing here" the familiar voice of John Wassail rang in his ears as he was, as usual, playing pool in the Vermuyden pub.

John and his crew had just arrived in the dock with a yacht which they had sailed from Norway to live on in England. It transpired that they would be in London over the August Bank holiday putting on a firework display in Docklands.

"If you will be there by then it would be great if you could accommodate the 'Walk the Plank' team, we will be happy to pay you a going rate" he proposed. This was sometime in June so it gave Rod the impetus to get Wylam ready to sail with a date to aim for which he achieved after the second North sea adventure.

It took them nearly a week to set the display up during which time they used Rod as a 'gofa'. They were a mad bunch and asked Rod if he minded them doing the odd line. "no problem!" he said although one of the other boaters told him, later, that if they had been raided he could have been in trouble. The explosives expert was an Irish lad with one leg. He had blown the other one off experimenting, probably, Rod thought, blowing up safes for the IRA.
Johnny was the quiet one so that when he asked if he and his girlfriend, Anna, could stay on in a cabin and contribute to the upkeep of the boat, Rod and Anne were only too pleased agree. Letting cabins to friends and family proved to be the saving solution to his financial problems after the hotel boat idea had turned out to be a non starter.

Sue King, the BW manager of Poplar Dock Marina, seemed to be one of the best and organised meetings in the Swan pub across the road from poplar Dock.

"You should come on to the committee" she invited but Rod just replied "No thanks I have been on enough committees to last me a lifetime". She did eventually rue the day when he eventually became involved but he just wanted a quiet life enjoying the company of Anne and fellow boaters.

"You are getting a name as a groper and a dirty old man" Anne warned him. He could not think it was entirely fair because he was just enjoying a bit of harmless flirting with the girls 'women' who seemed to be playfully teasing and encouraging him.
Maggie was the worst and on one occasion when there were a few of them playing pool in the pub and he was playing Mike, her partner, she had been persistently interfering with Rods shots. The final playful straw was when she actually grabbed the cue and ran off round the table with it.
"Mikey! Mikey!" she screamed as he caught her up and grabbed hold of her, "He grabbed my fanny!" Mike thought it was quite amusing having observed the whole thing but one or two of the others who only heard the screams thought the worst of him. Later he was told of verbal exchanges like the one from Brendan.

"I don't know what I would have done if he had grabbed my Gill like that". Rod could have assured him the there were no circumstances were he would have gone anywhere near his precious starchy Gill.
There was quite a cross section of people on the marina, nearly all working, not like the continuous cruisers on the canal who partly consisted of alkies, drug addicts and drop outs mixed in with a few employed and retired couples. Marina life was fun with parties, barbecues and the Swan. If you were feeling like company, real pub grub, a drink and pool, you could always just go across the road and it would be guaranteed that other boaters would be there.

It was, he felt, a bit like being in a 'Carry on' film. Anne joined in some times but was basically not a pub person although on one occasion, just to prove a point, she did drink him 'under the table' when she and Maggie had to virtually carry him back to the boat and put him to bed.
He thought that his luck was in but they just left him there 'alone and palely wondering!' so, after a few minutes he followed them back to the pub.

It was time for another change in the direction of his life. He had always wanted to traverse the European canals so he set about, with Anne, looking for a Dutch barge. The idea was to buy one and sail around the Dutch and French canals and then bring it back to the uk and sell it. They found a small Tjalk in the north of Holland and planned to bring her back except that Anne, after her experiences in the North sea, refused to accompany him. Undeterred he rounded up several volunteers from Poplar Dock and his new venture was under way.

the end

Made in the USA
Charleston, SC
28 February 2016